People
Are
~~Stoopid~~
~~Stewpid~~
Dumb

People Are ~~Stoopid~~ ~~Stewpid~~ Dumb

*A Humorous Approach to
Modern Social Problems*

BY: Alex P. Hewing

iUniverse, Inc.
Bloomington

People Are Dumb
A Humorous Approach to Modern Social Problems

iUniverse books may be ordered through booksellers or by contacting:

iUniverse
1663 Liberty Drive
Bloomington, IN 47403
www.iuniverse.com
1-800-Authors (1-800-288-4677)

ISBN: 978-1-4759-5960-4 (sc)
ISBN: 978-1-4759-5961-1 (ebk)

Library of Congress Control Number: 2012920569

Printed in the United States of America

iUniverse rev. date: 11/17/2012

CONTENTS

ACKNOWLEDGMENTS

I've been told that it's considered very orthodox to include a "Special Thanks" page in the beginning of your book. Well, I am anything but orthodox. But I guess a few justifiable shout outs couldn't hurt. First and foremost, I would like to thank whoever created Adderall. So, to whoever that person is, thank you for giving me the attention span to finally sit still and focus long enough to write a book. Next, I'd like to thank both of my parents. Without them, I wouldn't be here. Seriously, I wouldn't. I'm here because my mom and dad had sex, I'm guessing without a condom, which ultimately, led to me.

I would sincerely like to thank my father for giving me advice all throughout my life that I still use to this day. I would like to thank my mother for implanting her creative talents into me in my youth and encouraging me to never stop listening to 80's music. To one of my best friends in the world, Wayne Workman, I'd like to say, "I can't believe you stared at my balls like that". To Dr. Scott Holzer, I owe the very depth of my passion for education to you, my friend. I will always remember the valuable lessons you have instilled in me, and place the value of your words above almost any other. I will never be able to put a price on what you have given me (I mean, other than the cost of a typical three credit hour college class).

Let's see, am I forgetting anyone? Oh! I'm forgetting the most obvious thank you of all. I guess I should thank all of the stupid people out in the world for disgusting me to the point of writing a whole goddamn book about it. Without all of you, I would have no inspiration. Although, I think I would trade writing this book for getting to live in a better world.

PREFACE

This book is meant to be taken as a humorous collection of opinions supported by facts. This is not a book to be referenced for anyone writing a college paper. If you do that, you may end up getting an "F". Don't say I didn't warn you. **This book is not for anyone that does not have a good sense-of-humor.**

I've written that last part in bold so that you'll know that I'm serious. If you're the kind of person that gets your feelings hurt when someone says anything contrary to your opinion about religion, politics, abortion, etc., this book is not for you.

If that's the case, I appreciate you taking the time to read this far, but you're probably better off putting this book away now. At least if you stop reading now, you can avoid the hours you'll have to spend writing hate mail. And I can rest easy knowing that all the tires on my car won't be slashed tomorrow, and I won't be stoned to death while walking outside to grab the hate mail you sent me.

If you do have a good sense-of-humor and you want to keep reading, I applaud you for putting yourself out there and taking a chance. I would also like to take this time to apologize if my writing sucks. I do my very best to entertain people while trying to support my opinion on several subjects in the hopes that I can have a positive outcome on someone's previous idiotic thinking. The areas that I poke fun at are not meant to be taken offense to. Crude humor just happens to be one of the only ways in which I know how to reach people.

You may note that I support my opinions with several facts. The truth is, the facts are all crap that you can find online just like I did. If you want to see where I got the information from, you can do exactly what I did and perform an online search. That's where I got most of my information. In the end, everyone is going to believe whatever they want to believe anyway.

So if you like this book please let me know so that I can find out if there's a need for me to write a second book. If you don't like this book, my name is Matthew McConaughey, and you should feel free to send me all of the hate mail your little spiteful heart can conjure up. Pay no attention to who this book says the author is. Just please send your hate mail to Matthew McConaughey. I can't stand that Hollywood pig. Walking around with his six-pack abs, his fan club made up of 98% women and 2% homosexual men, and making millions of dollars starring in crappy movies (except for *The Lincoln Lawyer;* that one was legit). I know jealousy is unbecoming of me, but I can't help it.

I decided to write this book because I could no longer stand the stupid people in society projecting their ignorance to everyone else around them and forcing others to be subjected to their stupidity. What's even worse are the people that see it happening every day, know that it's wrong, but choose to do or say nothing about it. I decided I couldn't be a hypocrite, which meant that I needed to do something. I guess I should look on the bright side—As long as there stupid people in the world, I will always have something to write about.

For anyone that actually enjoys my book, or hates my book, I encourage you to write to me and tell me why. Here is my email: skepticism101@gmail.com I look forward to reading and answering as many emails as possible. Who knows? Maybe I'll even get to write a book called *Thanks for the Hate Mail.*

Maybe no one will ever read this. Or maybe only a few people will. Either way, it doesn't matter. I couldn't go on any longer standing idly by and not saying something. Thank you for making it this far into the book.

A Quote from the Roman Writer Dante Alghieri:

"Lasciate ogne speranza, voi ch'intrate"
(*Abandon all hope, ye who enter here*)

Translation: There's no turning back once you get passed this point, people. If you want to turn back, now is your chance.

-Alex P. Hewing

Introduction

First things first, I am not a writer. I have never written anything that was of any significance, and I am writing this not to criticize, argue, or even anger anyone. Rather, I hope my thoughts and views will be both an eye-opening experience and entertaining. There are so many areas that I'm going to discuss that it would be pointless for me to try to describe every area of the book right now. But don't worry this book is based on a thesis. The thesis of which is probably something like: we need more education; we need to stop racism and prejudice; religion is dumb; you get the idea, right?

If anyone is reading this that carries an extremely high level of education with them, you will be happy to know that this book is a colloquial first-person perspective analysis, debating some of the most prevalent problems that the world experiences, in a thesis-based format. For anyone that knows what that last bit actually means, you'll figure out, in the first few pages of this chapter, just how full of shit I really am. If you're worried that you're reading a book about social problems from an uneducated writer with no credibility, you can relax. The truth is—although I am finishing my undergraduate degree in sociology, I've been studying social problems through interaction and proper documented research for years. If I had to guess, I would say that most people have been doing the same. The difference is they either don't realize it, or they choose to not do anything about it.

On a serious note, some of the issues I will be discussing are the most debated arguments and opposing forces that have been around for thousands of years. So, it should make for a really offensive, controversial book. I'm not a novelist, by the way. I wish I were, but I'm not. I don't possess the descriptive tongue.

It would more than likely take me 10 years to be able to write an average-length novel because I would have to learn how to describe my characters and scenery correctly. Novelists can describe a piece of fruit to the point that you can close your eyes and see it perfectly and even taste it. But to me, I guess, an orange tastes like an orange and a banana tastes like . . . . yellow. If you didn't laugh at that, don't worry. I'm sure there is bound to be at least one joke somewhere in this book that you'll laugh at.

Oh, and if you're looking for a large, classroom-style history lesson, you're reading the wrong book. My ideas may seem naïve and overly-optimistic to most. But hey, I never claimed to know everything or be perfect. On that note, I would like to share some of my thoughts and ideas with you on why I think people are dumb.

CHAPTER 1

Introducing . . . . Dumb People

People are stupid. I'm not suggesting that intelligence has anything to do with ignorance. I understand, and I hope you also understand, that ignorance is a lack of knowledge in any particular area. But man, people really are stupid.

I grew up writing poetry from about the age of 14 and just kept writing. It wasn't until I was about 28 years old that I even began writing anything else. As I began writing this book, I noticed several of the poems I was writing coincided with my thoughts throughout the book. For this reason, several of my poems, although not even a fraction of all that I have written, are included as they are discussed in the book.

I have always been an extremely sarcastic, loud, and outgoing person. I'll admit it. I love everyone's eyes being on me. I'm a natural attention whore. I can't help it. I'm also just as guilty of having my dumb moments as anyone else in the world. I'll explain what I mean. One time when I was a kid, I was being my usual loud, sarcastic, funny self when someone told me I was "naturally charismatic". Unfortunately, I didn't know what it meant so I responded how any teenaged American boy would. I said, "Fuck you". How dumb did I sound? Some guy I didn't even know paid me a compliment, and I replied by throwing a derogatory phrase at him. Sounds pretty typical.

I chose to reference my own life experience because it demonstrates how easily it can happen. Society's initial reaction is almost always to lash out and separate from whatever we don't understand, rather than simply learn from it. Thus, the perpetuation of stupidity among society continues to live on.

I began getting more and more into writing this book when I took a class at my local community college. One of my professors there,

Dr. Scott Holzer, opened my mind up to a wonderment I had never realized was lying dormant the entire time, my passion for education. It was quite strange and equally ironic because while in high school which was practically 10 years before I said over and over again, "When I get done with high school I am done with school for good".

I suppose the time was different in my life. Studying because you are told to is not the same as studying on your own because you want to. And college is exactly that. You are paying to go to college, one way or another. If you don't want to be there, you don't need to be. Perhaps that's why I sometimes stand bewildered at the idea of people that go to college and either drop out right away or fail because of a lack of effort.

While in my Ancient and Medieval Civilizations class with Dr. Holzer (who I now simply call Scott, as we are friends outside of his class at this point) I began having questions answered for me that I had been lingering on my whole life but simply never had the drive to investigate on my own. Scott was a professor unlike any I ever had before. He was a middle-aged looking man, clean-shaven with the stereotypical glasses that a man of his position and stature would wear. His expertise and passion for history was made obvious by the small library of history books of all sorts filling up one whole side of his office. His teaching style was both entertaining and informative. In my eyes, he was the reason teachers should become teachers.

Scott would begin to go off on a rant almost every class pertaining to whatever piece of history we were discussing that day. His passion for history was so clearly depicted that a blind, deaf, idiot could have seen it. Ironically, I received the lowest grade to date in his class, but I also learned more in his class than I have in any other class before or after. That's one of those fun facts that I enjoy telling people when I discuss the value of education and the emphasis of understanding the material as well as receiving a passing grade.

Scott hated it when people would project fallacies and display them as the absolute truth. I'm sure that's a fairly normal trait among history professors, but with him it was obvious. I'll tell you what I mean.

We were discussing the Greek and Persian Wars and got to a point of discussing the legendary Spartans. As soon as he mentioned the Spartans, you would have thought the whole class just drank an energy drink at the same time. Everybody's hand went up almost immediately.

People were asking questions left and right. Unfortunately, most of the questions revolved around the film *300* that had recently been released to the big screen. Man, Scott had a field day dissecting that movie and separating fact from fiction for all of his students.

He tore that movie apart. He wanted everyone to know that just because there's a Hollywood movie about it, that doesn't make it completely accurate. In all honesty, it usually means the opposite because the truth can typically ruin the success of a movie because fiction is more fun and much easier to keep you eating popcorn, as opposed to the truth, which is that the Spartans were:

1) Gay; I'm sorry, but yes, it's true.
2) Owned thousands of slaves that did all of their trades and work. That explains why the Spartans were capable of being the best-trained military of their time because they didn't have anything else to do; and . . . .
3) Were, in fact, accompanied by approximately 4,000-5,000 other soldiers during the actual Battle of Thermopylae including the Arcadian, Mycenaean, and Corinthian.

However, these facts make the movie far less attractive to the general populous. Which really sucks because all that says to me is that society isn't interested in the truth. They're just interested in eating popcorn. Long story short, by the end of Scott's class, I was well on my way in my quest for knowledge, education, understanding, and writing this book.

Speaking of war, please enjoy the first few poems in this book that deal with history and war.

Thermopylae

With valor in numbers abroad they marched
When life was a luxury that none could afford
And the others before fell like cattle
With bodies aching, starved and parched
They walked fearless ahead with their hearts lying poured
These brave men created for the heat of battle
Their king was one whose strength was unbound
His service was to his country and his men
And his name was heard beyond all others known
His blade bore death as he screamed aloud
Standing at the front he leads his condemned
Already convinced he will never return home
Battling down the god king's force
With thunderous battle cries that would wake the dead
And the blood of thousands still upon their blades
The pompous tyrant finds a hole in their course
Outflanking the three hundred forces ahead
And mark the defiant king's land enslaved
And in the end it was few standing against many
Every man endowed with courage and pride
And every man dying beside their king
Their numbers were small but their hearts counted plenty
May history always remember their tithe
For those that died at Thermopylae

<u>Times of Light</u>

There will be times of light and yes
There will be times in the dark
Times when men will question their lives
And the value in their scars
There will be times of light and yes
There will be times of hate
Where emotions run like Arabian steeds
And care only to eradicate
There will be times of light and yes
There will be times of pain
Times when the trials of the world
Will seem to fall as beads of rain
There will be times of light and yes
Times where our patience is tried
But believe in me my band of brothers
I will never leave your side

History

While delving into history if you stop and admire
You can see more than just rubble and rock
You can see monuments of kings, the gladiators' great ring
And halls where the first emperor had walked
You can see statues that were formed in a time long before
With tools we would laugh at and throw away
You can see gardens that hang as long as the city
That no one would dare duplicate today
Look closer at the stones that are older than we understand
And you will find they were unmovable by man
And lifted so high where no man could reach
In a time when technology was the strength in your hand
If you stop and stare you may find you appreciate
The names of our loved ones carved in stones
And perhaps you will show more love for the fallen
Because history is more than simply dust and bones
We need not worry about tomorrow
Because time will take its toll and fade
Instead live for each moment and respect the past
For every moment history is being made

After I got out of Scott's class, the days quickly turned into months. I soon began studying on my own. From that point on, any time I didn't know the answer to something I wanted to research it and look it up for myself. Part of that stemmed from another good buddy from my past, who for the sake of anonymity, we will call "Fren Dove Mine". There was one thing in particular Fren said to me when I asked him a question that always stuck with me. Any time I would ask him a question, he would say, "I don't know; why don't you look it up and get back to me". I still use that line to this day.

He knew the answer almost every time; I can almost guarantee it. But that wasn't the point. The point was getting me to research something on my own. And not only that, but conducting good research so that I could know for certain the information that I researched was accurate.

Moral of the story: Never trust a donkey crossing the road on a Tuesday. What did you expect? I'm a crap author, and I'm writing crap.

CHAPTER 2

Indoctrination? What's That?

Indoctrination! Indoctrination! Indoctri-Fucking-Nation! It's an extremely powerful word that the majority of the populous is unable to define. So let's start there.

Indoctrination—1) teaching to accept a system of thought uncritically

To help aid in the clarification of this word, indoctrination is also synonymous with the words: brainwash, program, and propagandize. If you don't know what those words mean you can simply look them up in the dictionary to help you define them. If you still can't figure it out after that you're probably from a place where people are indoctrinated into never researching the term indoctrination. In the hopes of helping you understand the ideas behind indoctrination, please read this poem that was written specifically for this section of the book.

<u>Indoctrinated</u>

Nothing you can say will ever shake my faith
Regardless of the proof, I am in a resolute state
Placing logic before me will never raise my doubt
My choice is placed in something that I know nothing about
I should not explore ideas based on my own free-thinking
Because questioning "The One" can only lead to reasoning
You will find me hating those that my father tells me to hate
He told me if you are different, it's OK to discriminate
We will follow blindly without any questions raised
And never lift an eyebrow to what is offered in exchange
You would call me a zealot, and I would have to agree
Because I choose to remain uneducated and follow what others believe

Indoctrination happens all the time, all around us. It's in the way you speak, your work ethic, and the number of times you have to check the locks on the doors in your home. FYI, that last one is only in the event that your parent suffers from obsessive compulsive disorder. It's right in front of all of our ignorant, blissful faces, and we are none-the-wiser. Every time parents take their children to a particular church, the children are being indoctrinated. Every time a racist person passes on their views of why the white man is responsible for keeping the black man down for so long, people are being indoctrinated.

Sometimes indoctrination manifests itself in ways that far more extreme and dangerous such as: the military brainwashing soldiers, racism, prejudice, religion, and some of the most notorious organizations of today like the KKK, the Aryan Brotherhood, the Black Gorillas, the LRA, the Mexican Mafia, every mafia that has ever existed, honestly. Not to mention the ever-increasing number of street gangs.

The danger of indoctrination is that we don't realize it while it's happening, and it is going to happen rather we want it to or not. It's an unstoppable force, like a roundhouse kick from Chuck Norris. What we as a society can change is what we allow ourselves to be indoctrinated into. Indoctrination can become so symbolic and integrated that it essentially becomes an indestructible idea, especially if it has a large enough following.

However, the problem is that most people don't even know what indoctrination is. That's why they never stop and realize it when it's happening. This is why education and eliminating ignorance is so important. Without it, society will just continue down the path of blind hatred and corruption. But that's enough talk about politics. Let's get serious.

If someone you don't even know walks up to you and begins to ask you to come join his cult, church, gay rights movement, picketing of Wal-Mart (which has no effect on their sales by the way), please stop and take a step back to think before you commit to anything. Do some research before you start to give up your freedom to think. People say you should question authority. I say, fuck that; you should question people. That means everybody. After all, some groups that people get involved in aren't so easy to get out of once you get in.

People are easily led because they're always looking to belong. Everyone's so goddamn afraid of being rejected by the other members of society that they are willing to do anything to fit in, including becoming an apostate (giving up one's own beliefs, in case you were wondering). That's known as social conformity, which I will discuss at the end of this book. Ironically, the people that are made into pariahs by society and aren't connected with any of the groups that are known for their negative indoctrination can end up forming their own organizations and begin creating and handing down their own forms of indoctrination, often times aimed against the people who rejected them. Can anyone see a pattern forming here?

Indoctrination is probably the most prevalent from parents to their children because that's who children spend the majority of their time with. It's one thing to have strong personal convictions about what you believe is right and wrong. But when you force religion, political stance, or prejudice on your kids, you take away their most basic freedoms. It's a sensitive issue to discuss. I know that if you try to tell me that I'm raising my children wrong, my first impulse would be to tell you to mind your own business. I would probably also want to yell a few vulgar words, and I would have to do my best to refrain from acting on both of those impulses. Most people consider themselves to be genuinely good parents that know what is best for their children. I think most people are sheep, but I'm saying that about people in general. To the sheep out there reading this, you guys really need to stop being sheep. Oh, I'm sorry. You probably didn't understand that did you? Let me try that again in your native sheep tongue. Baaa . . . . Baaa. Baaa. Baaa . . . . Baaa. Baaa. There, that should have cleared up any confusion.

Indoctrination needs to be monitored. Society needs widespread disclosure on the subject if we ever hope to learn and grow. More specifically, people need to be made aware of its existence so that they can spot it when it is being improperly used. In its most common form, indoctrination is used to manipulate people. It always seems to be the most innocent, uncorrupted people that are indoctrinated into hatred too. By innocent, I mean uneducated and ignorant in the ways of the world. I honestly think of many of these individuals are victims that are being taken advantage of because they don't know any better.

It comes down to having an opinion and not being afraid to express it. No one should have to follow someone else' opinions throughout their whole life. I think what upsets me the most is when people are indoctrinated at such a young age that they have no defense against it. Those people will never have the choice to say, "You know what? I think I disagree with that". Something as small as that will never even be an option for these people because they were never made to understand that they have a choice.

My mind just can't get over the fact that there is a large number of people that see nothing wrong with telling their children, "This is the way it is. This is the way it has always been. Anyone who has an opinion that says otherwise is wrong, and it's our job to let them know it". How, may I ask, is that supposed to promote understanding? That's like having a blind man pointing a finger at the guilty party in a murder trial.

For many of the dangerous, indoctrinated individuals, it is their closed-mindedness that also poses a huge threat. They're blind. If you are so set in your ways that you are not even open to listening to something that contradicts your opinion, you might as well consider yourself a slave. It must be a comfort though, when you realize you never knew your freedom was stolen from you, because you never knew you had it from the beginning.

It's redundant and never-ending. People want to be accepted. I do, you do, the weirdo at the grocery store with that.... half-mustache-thing, that I haven't quite figured out. Everybody wants to be accepted. But to blindly agree to start organizing with something you know nothing about is ludicrous and dangerous. Now it's time to talk about some the previous groups I mentioned and why it's so important to know what you're getting yourself into.

I wish there was a way for me to put my usual humorous spin on the next three chapters you're about to read. Unfortunately, the groups I am about to describe are so ruthless that I don't think I could place any sort of a positive outlook on their actions or their behaviors. Not to mention the fact that if I made these groups seem amusing or entertaining for any reason, it might send readers the wrong message. I don't think I'm being too sarcastic when I say that I wouldn't piss on a member of any one of these groups if they were on fire. The worst part of it all is that these groups are only a fraction of the sick and inhumane organizations in the world today.

Moral of the story: Everyone wants to be accepted. But choosing to be accepted by a group that you know nothing about is like a deaf guy picking out his favorite song.

CHAPTER 3

Caucasians in the Underground

Compared to the Aryan Brotherhood, the members of the Ku Klux Clan are practically Girl Scouts. The Aryan Brotherhood (AB) is one of the largest white supremacist groups in the U.S. The AB originated in San Quentin Prison. The gang commonly uses the Norse religion practices as a cover to maintain their regularly scheduled meetings to discuss group activity. They are well-organized within their system, dividing jobs and titles. They have an actual council, hold elections, follow strict rules to the letter, and even punish their own members for violating their established rules. The group has over 15,000 members both inside and outside of the prison system. If anybody out there thinks these mother fuckers are the real deal, I suggest you look at some of the gang's historical facts.

1) Several of the older AB members went as far as to learn sign-language in an effort to communicate their messages covertly.

2) The organization's membership operates on a "blood in/blood out" system meaning that to become a member a recruit must successfully murder another prisoner to enter the gang. Likewise, if a member wants out, there is only one way, and I think you can figure that out on your own.

3) The AB focuses its activities on organized crime such as racketeering, drug trafficking, extortion, prostitution, and contract-killing.

4) Members have also reportedly used cryptograms to code their messages, including a 400-year-old Sir Francis Scott Bacon binary alphabet system. So, you can bet, these guys know their shit, and they are not stupid.

5) The gang might make up only 1% of the prison population, but that 1% is responsible for 26% of all murders in federal prisons.

Moral of the story: If you don't want to be forced to choose sides and commit terrible actions that tear away at the fabric of humanity, don't do something to end up in prison.

CHAPTER 4

Latinos with Attitude

The next group that I will be discussing is the Mexican Mafia, or La eMe (pronounced emmay, as in, the letter M in Spanish), as the members are commonly called. The Mexican Mafia originated as an entirely prison-based gang. Currently however, the gang has just as much influence on the outside as they do on the inside of the prison system. The gang members are noted to have the number "13" tattooed on their body somewhere (the letter M is the 13th letter in the alphabet). Another marking denoting gang members is a tattoo of a black hand. Me personally, I would think that it should be a brown colored hand, but I'm guessing that it's difficult to find ink in that color inside of a prison.

These guys seriously take their work home with them. They are involved in a variety of criminal acts on both sides of the bars. They get the majority of their business via drug distributors on the inside and outside of prison systems.

The Mexican Mafia is currently an ally of the Aryan Brotherhood, especially for the white prison gang's notorious connections with contract killing. The gang's primary involvement, again, being drug trafficking on the inside and outside; that doesn't mean this heavy handed prison gang is against committing other crimes such as murder, and not just the murder of other gangs; they murder their own members if they can get a vote from three other senior members of the gang to do so. Not only that, these die-hard, Latino thugs have a rule that states that the person who initially sponsored the gang member being killed has to be the one to commit the murder. That's why the gang goes by the rule "Blood In, Blood Out".

The only way to become a member of La eMe is by committing a murder, and the only way out of the gang is to be killed. Make no mistake, these Latin Kings of the prison world, only have one major Latin gang rival, La Nuestra Familia (Our Family). La Nuestra Familia is an ally of the African-American prison gang known as The Black Gorillas. Suffice is to say, Latinos definitely have their own reserved seat at the wrongful indoctrination dinner table.

Moral of the story: These guys are linked up with the guys from the last chapter. You do the math.

CHAPTER 5

From Uganda, With Shame

The Lord's Resistance (LRA) is the last group of the three I am going to discuss. In my opinion, their actions are almost too disgusting to think about. The LRA is responsible for atrocities most governments would declare martial law over. They are led and founded by a man named Joseph Kony who hails from northern Uganda. One of the things that make the organization seem more disgusting than others is that the rebels that make up the LRA state that they fight for a government built and run on the Biblical Ten Commandments. How very virtuous of this group to establish an organization that is built on the Ten Commandments to commit acts such as: killing members of humanitarian groups attempting to give aid to Ugandan countrymen; the abduction of thousands of children from their families; kidnapping and raping young women and girls and using them as sex slaves; and selling young women off as slave labor.

Some of the male LRA prisoners are used for manual slave labor. Several adult males are given the ultimatum of joining the LRA's military forces or being killed. But probably the most notorious action that I can mention the LRA being responsible for is thousands of children throughout their time being brainwashed into being used as guards and soldiers for their militia. The LRA promises the children all of the money, power, and freedom they could ever desire by joining their militia and becoming part of a new family. It sounds like a good deal to the children, as long as the children are willing to kill other men, women, and even children that try to escape captivity or go as far as to kill their own families if need be. I wish I could tell you that the children were smart enough not to accept the offer. But the truth is seldom easy to hear. I implore anyone who doubts the validity of this information to research it on their own. There are several websites you can reference for yourself.

All of these groups have two things in common; they are all guilty of using indoctrination as a means to commit crimes, and they all make me want to give up hope on humanity. It's up to us to educate ourselves, stand together, and ensure that groups like this are taken down and never allowed to be created again. I'm a realist though, so I realize that idea is well-beyond achievable at this point. What I do know is that if a group such as the LRA ever came and took my two daughters from me and indoctrinated them into a life of slavery or placed them in the sex trade, I would feel no remorse committing acts upon them so harsh and sickening that Satan himself would be handing over his thrown to me without thinking twice. I'm sorry. I can't think about situations like that and not get upset. If you actually knew what I was thinking of doing to them right now, you'd have to take a bath, while you rocked back and forth sucking your thumb.

Now that I'm good and pissed off, what do you say we lighten the mood a little bit? As I previously mentioned, indoctrination is practically inevitable in society. But indoctrination doesn't always have to be a bad thing. A good example of indoctrination that is common and generally not dangerous is non-conflicting family traditions, like spending Christmas at a certain grandparents' house every year.

Academic indoctrination is usually OK too. Every student that is enrolled and actively participates academically is eventually going to become indoctrinated with the way things are run at whatever educational institution they happen to be attending. Rather it's grade school, high school, or college, it doesn't matter; it still happens. One day you're a free thinker, capable of making your own choices with no influence from an outside stimulus. The next day you're reciting whatever pledge the school lives by without even thinking about it. It's kind of like a Catholic reciting the Hail Mary four times before bed every night. That person isn't thinking about what they are actually saying. They're just doing it because it's what they've been taught.

In short, stop forcing beliefs on people, especially children. Beliefs are dangerous. Let someone come to their own decision about where to place their religious beliefs or which political party to favor. We should be able to trust our children to make the right choices through education. The more pressure we place on children to "Do what I say, or else", the more they will rebel against their parental role models.

Moral of the story: Anyone horrible enough to commit the acts that the LRA has committed deserves to have every bone in their bodies broken. And they would receive no sympathy while they lie there suffering. Not even from Satan. Satan would just look the other way, whistling, and pretending he didn't see or hear anything.

CHAPTER 6

I Feel Bad, but It's True

Disclaimer: Hey! Wake up! We're about to talk about some serious shit. So before we begin diving into this touchy subject, let's all be realists here agreed? Quite often there is some truth to the origin of negative stereotypes. The stereotypes aren't just popping out of nowhere like Janet Jackson's breast after a wardrobe malfunction, are they? That doesn't make negative stereotyping OK, but it's a fact. It's also going to be extremely important through the duration of this chapter to remind you constantly not to carry a thin skin.

That being said, every man and woman on the earth is responsible for their own choices. If I make a bad choice, I have to live with the consequences. I choose to live my life the best that I can with as much respect equally to every human being. I choose to live this way because that is how I would want to be treated by everyone else. It's called being civil. Let's take a look at that word, stereotype real quick.

Stereotype: **1)** A conventional, formulaic, usu. oversimplified opinion, conception, or belief. **2)** One, as a person, group, event, or issue that is thought to typify or conform to an unvarying pattern or manner lacking any individuality. **3)** A metal printing plate cast from a matrix that is molded from a raised printing surface, as type.

You know, when they word it like that, it doesn't make stereotyping sound all that bad. (OK, so that third one has nothing to do with what we're talking about. I just felt the need to include it since it was in the dictionary)

Negative stereotypes are the worst. We all know them. We see and hear about them all the time projected by the media, the government, and Hollywood. I could probably write a completely separate book called "101 Stereotypes", but I'm just going to be going over a few of them and discuss why they are wrong and need to be stopped.

From a philosophical point of view, not all stereotypes are bad. Let me explain; calm down. There are different stereotypes. The main two forms of stereotypes are physical stereotypes and negative personified stereotypes.

Physical stereotypes are a characteristic of someone's genetic makeup. Ergot: No one can change their genetic makeup. I mean . . . . Not without some hefty advances in science and medicine and a pretty big checkbook. Negative stereotypes on the other hand are just pretty much wrongful labeling of a person or group without the appropriate representation of said depiction. Now, the list is long and abhorrent, so I'm only including a few. Please try to save your hate mail until the end so you can include all of the ways in which you were offended. Now then, on with the blind hatred.

Physical Stereotypes:

1) Scandinavians—large, Viking-size, blonde hair, blue eyes.
2) Jews—longer than usual noses, Mediterranean skin tone, extremely, curly hair "the Jew-Fro".
3) Caucasians—ummmm . . . . Anything and everything because we're a mix of everybody else.
4) African-Americans—Bulkier than usual noses, larger lips, a more Neanderthal physique (which makes sense to me considering Africa was home to the first humans on Earth, but that's a whole other argument), afro hair, and the "ghetto booty".
5) Indians (the real kind, from India)—Dark hair, dark skin . . . . You know now that I think about it, trying to describe the typified person from India is difficult when you're not allowed to make note of the Hindu religion or use the negative stereotypes of the "7-11 Slurpee" voice, the dots on their foreheads, etc. You know what? How's this? The guys from *Indiana Jones and the Temple of Doom.*
6) British—Basically your typical Caucasians with ghastly teeth that look like the toothpaste factories closed down, and they just never bothered to reopen them. For that matter, I wonder if Steve Buscemi is secretly British? I mean his teeth are just wrecked, aren't they?

P.S. Steve, if you ever happen to read this, I want you to know that I think you're an amazing actor, and I love your movies. Don't ever change buddy. Armageddon kicked ass!

These are just a few of the examples of physical stereotypes. Again, they are obviously not always accurate which is why it is unfair to label any one individual with any of them.

Final Disclaimer: Every one of the preceded stereotypes and the following stereotypes are completely wrong and wrong to label other people with. If you had difficulty with the physical stereotypes I strongly suggest you move ahead to the next chapter. Chances are however, it won't matter. I'm sure the next chapter is just as difficult and controversial as this one. So if you've made it this far, you're probably OK.

Negative Personified Stereotypes

4) Average American Caucasians—Fast-food franchising yuppies, morbidly obese (but I think that one's there for a reason), overindulgent, self-gratifying, capitalists, carrying multiple guns in the hopes of one day fulfilling their dream of getting the chance to shoot all of the people they were told to hate while going through their life.

5) Puerto Ricans—Are lucky to fit in one shower a week.

6) Italians—Are apparently all in the mob one way or another; only eat spaghetti and lasagna; and they think they have better hair than everybody else on the planet.

7) Greeks—Not in the mob, but are positive they have better hair than the Italians.

8) African-Americans—Thieves, crooks, hoodlums, you get the point; all muscle-no brains; they all seem to only eat chicken, watermelon, and drink grape soda; they drive pimped out cars with $1,000 sound systems and $600 spinners on a car that doesn't have car insurance for some reason; drug users and drug dealers; they all feel the need to have their teeth made of "bling", they're all in gangs; living on welfare because they can't find or hold down a job. Uh, let's see. What are some of the other ridiculous ones that are out there? Oh! They're all in prison or just got out; and none

of them have a father because they're all deadbeat-dads. There, I think that about covers it.

9)   Southern-American Caucasians—Here goes . . . . They're all racist; married to their cousin, sister, or the sister of their cousin which is still really weird; uneducated (not uneducated like they can't use a noun and a verb properly in a sentence; uneducated like they don't even know what the Hell a noun and a verb is); they all drive trucks with big mud tires and gun racks to hold all of the guns. You know . . . . Obviously, that makes sense, right? It's nearly impossible to focus on what they are ever saying because of the tobacco spit dribbling down their face; they sit around and admire their yard furniture (i.e. the engines from the previous three trucks they took apart to try and get one of them up and running); and they've memorized the Redneck Comedy Tour. BOOM!!! Take that, southern states.

10) Mexicans—They are . . . . lazy, grass cutting, low-rider driving, gang members that all have 10 kids to help increase the number of jobs in America they can steal from the people I just mentioned in #4.

11) Columbians—Basically, Mexican wannabes that make damn good cocaine and coffee.

12) French Men—Think they're better than everyone else in the world; they shower more than the Puerto Ricans but smell just as bad; they all hate American men for some reason. I have no idea why. Honestly, I don't. I'm not even kidding. I can't figure it out. I've been doing the history and the math, and I have no idea what they're problem is.

13) French Women—Apparently ran out of razors some time back in the dark ages, which explains the hairy pits.

14) Russians—"VODKA!!!!! LET'S FIGHT!!!!!"

15) Irish—"Hennessy!!!!! LET'S FIGHT!!!!!!"

16) Germans—"JAGERMEISTER!!!!! LET'S FIGHT, AND THEN IF THERE IS STILL TIME WE CAN GO KILL ALL OF THE JEWS!!!!! (All right, so that last part was kind of taken out of context, but I just couldn't resist)

17) Native-Americans—"LET'S OPEN A CASINO AND SMOKE A WHOLE SHITLOAD OF WEED!!!!!"

18) Jewish—"LET'S GO KILL JESUS OF NAZARETH, TAKE OVER THE WORLD BANK, AND THEN NEVER SPEND ANOTHER DIME AS LONG AS WE LIVE!!!!!"

19) Catholic Priests—"Now that I'm done molesting little boys, who needs to confess their sins and have to do five hairy males . . . . I mean, Hail Maries." I think I might actually be going to Hell after that one. But admit it, you're laughing which means you're going to Hell with me.

20) The Chinese—"Guess what I did today? I stole 10 American jobs and worked 16 hours in a factory that will fire me as soon as I complain or cut my finger on one of the machines."

21) The Japanese—"I'm crashing my plane into Pearl Harbor right now."

22) Muslims—"I'm crashing my plane into the World Trade Center right now."

23) Republicans—"Every Democrat sucks and hates America."

24) Democrats—"Every Republican sucks and hates America."

25) Pro-Life—"Who is going to hold the baby's hand during the abortion?"

26) Pro-Choice—"Who is going to hold YOUR hand while I'm killing you?"

Sadly, that is only a few of the negative stereotypes out there. OK, for anyone still reading, I commend your bravery through this vigorous display of unscrupulous, negative connotation. Now that I've gotten that out of the way, I'd like to remind everyone that, regardless of how funny it is, it is wrong to negatively stereotype anyone (even though it's natural and we all do it). Stereotyping takes away every man and woman's very individuality and it's unfair to judge someone and label someone when you don't know anything about who they are as a person.

The moral of this story: If you don't want anyone labeling you with another group, and thus negating all individual characteristics, why would you do it to anyone else?

CHAPTER 7

Defining Lines

I think it's important to differentiate between racism and prejudice. Racism is when someone hates a specific ethnicity or color, for whatever the reason. Essentially, without ever having met someone before, they presume to pass judgment on everyone of that race because of the color of their skin. Racists are unaware that who everyone is as a person has nothing at all to do with the color of their skin. If both your parents are white, you're going to be white.

Racism—prejudice or discrimination based on race.

Prejudice—1) **a.** an adverse opinion or judgment formed beforehand or without full knowledge or complete examination of the facts. **b.** a preconceived idea or preference. **2)** the act or state of holding unreasonable preconceived judgments or convictions. **3)** irrational hatred or suspicion of a specific group, race, or religion. **4)** detriment to one resulting from the preconceived and unfavorable conviction of another or others.

A prejudice is passing judgment over a specific group without regards to individuality, but it is not necessarily derived from a racial standpoint. For example, correctional officers hating offenders for being offenders without knowing anything about the individual is a form of prejudice. A devout Christian hating me for being an Atheist is another example. When I speak to people, often the best way that I have found to explain the correlation between racism and prejudice is that a racist will always be a prejudiced person because they are passing judgment on an entire group. A prejudiced person may not always be a racist because their race may have nothing to do with the prejudice. You could even simplify it even further by saying someone hating everyone wearing white gloves is demonstrating a form of prejudice.

I constantly talk to people about being open-minded and accepting of others. A lot of people laugh at me or look at me awkwardly when I tell them I am a hypocrite because I am prejudiced against anyone who is prejudiced. I only say that to help illustrate my point.

Much of the prejudice and racism in the world comes from negative stereotypes. If you are judging an entire group based off of one isolated incident, you're **FUCKING** wrong. In case you are someone who can't figure out if you are wrongly judging others, here's a nice, simple checklist to help you figure out if you're a prejudiced douche-bag.

1) If you're a Caucasian and you see a black guy and have to run home real quick to grab your white hood;
2) If you see a guy from Guatemala and get pissed off thinking about all of the illegal <u>Mexicans</u> in the U.S.;
3) If you're an African-American who sees a white guy and feels the need to beat him senseless because some random white guy called you the "N" word once;
4) If you see a Chinese person and walk up screaming at them about taking American jobs, and then find out that the person is from Okinawa;
5) If you see a Middle-Eastern person begin to board your plane and you say to yourself, "Fuck this. Florida's not going anywhere, and I can always catch a later flight".

If you answered "Yes" to any of these questions, you're a prejudiced douche-bag. And where does prejudice and racism stem from? From ignorance. Ignorance, the deadly plague that has been mercilessly crippling society since the dinosaurs. I'm sure the Brontosaurus made prejudiced remarks all the time like . . . ."Every Tyrannosaur will steal your TV and won't even think twice about knocking over an oasis at gun point".

That last anecdote might be funny, but the truth is ignorance is dangerous, and it's everywhere. I wish more people could see when they are being cruel. And not the kind of cruel found in my writing. I mean actual cruelty. Being forced to bear witness to the ignorance all around us in society day after day severely takes its toll on me. It makes me sadder than a generic cereal box at a grocery store that gets passed up every day and has to watch all of the name brand cereal boxes go home with happy families. It's unfair. It's tragic. And it's wrong . . . . The ignorance among society thing, not the cereal thing. Now that your attention is pointed as far from the original topic as mine is, please enjoy some of my thoughts on racism and prejudice.

A Blind Man's Cause

How many people hate each other for reasons unexplained?
How many could learn from one another if they could open up eyes?
Every day I am forced to pander to those who blindly hate
But I will not break, not budge, nor fight a blind man's cause
Vicious words from animals that bicker in ignorance
"How can you not hate all of them", they would ask
"They are all worthless and deserve to be wiped out"
But I will not break, nor budge, nor fight a blind man's cause
At first I was angry at how blind their ignorance had made them
But now I see it differently; my anger is now my pity
Because they will spend their whole life walking blindly and alone
But I will not break, nor budge, nor fight a blind man's cause

The United States of Diversity

I am black, and I am proud
I represent the perseverance of Dr. King
I will never feel shame for the color of my skin
My freedom soars with unbreakable wings
I am brown, and I am proud
I am a shining example of Juarez himself
I will never feel shame for the color of my skin
Race has no bearing on values or wealth
I am white, and I am proud
I carry Lincoln's message when I shake my neighbors' hands
I will never feel shame for the color of my skin
I will uphold our Declaration from which we began
I am an American, and I am proud
I will never let my actions bring my virtue disgrace
I will never feel shame for the color of my skin
Because my virtue is not something you can see in my face

<u>The Color of the Mind</u>

Bold words from those that feel the need to cause pain
Senseless lashing leaving so many slain
In crowded rooms with others where the game is played
Silent tension makes every man among them a slave
Ever long it will last in the bond of brothers
The passing of hate from one generation to another
Fighting and bickering for reasons unknown
Carrying on a legacy of hearts made of stone
How pigment changes the views of men is still a mystery
And should I have the power I would erase it from history
To my left and right are equals and in both I will confide
Though different in their faces, I would proudly stand beside

Blind Eyes

I would rather walk the earth with blind eyes than live with prejudice in my heart.

I would rather choose my friends by the times that we've shared, rather than by the color of their skin.

I would rather reach out a hand and not care what language they spoke,

And let my actions be a universal language.

I would rather offer peace of mind in a time of a racist war, to show everyone that we are all alike.

I would rather fight a war in the dark so that I may not see the face of the man protecting me.

I would rather spend my life learning from other cultures rather than trying to make them adopt all of ours.

I would rather know my family is still going to be my family regardless of who I decide to marry.

Wouldn't the world be a better place if we could all walk the earth with blind eyes?

The long and short of it, no one has the right to hate someone based solely on their race, color, religion, etc. You can probably fill in the rest of that with a typical, corporate "equal opportunity" class, so I'm just going to leave it at that. Wait . . . . I take that back. The only person that's allowed to hold a prejudice is Chuck Norris. Did you know, Chuck Norris is so tough he doesn't look left and right before he tells prejudice jokes? (Thank you Chuck Norris facts) Luckily, we all know that's just a joke. Chuck Norris would never be a racist because that would mean that Chuck Norris isn't perfect. And we all know that Chuck Norris is so perfect that the word perfect wants to be like Chuck Norris when it grows up.

Moral of the story: Unless you're Chuck Norris you shouldn't be racist.

CHAPTER 8

Slavery Sucked

Slavery is one of the most insulting acts that mankind has ever had the fortitude to conjure up. Forcing people to work against their will, often upon the threat of death is ethically and morally wrong. Of course, the people working against their will is pretty common in the prison system. But again, those people were found to be guilty of breaking the law. Now, that might be something that I get into more detail about in my next book, but not right now.

I can't even count the number of reasons why slavery is wrong. First of all, slavery is a crime against humanity. It's like letting Paris Hilton play professional football. The fact that people were ever able to think slavery is OK is nauseating. But what I find even more appalling is that there are still people to this day, in the U.S. that thinks slavery never should have been abolished. I don't think I'm being too far-fetched saying that the majority of those people think that the history books are telling the wrong side of the story when they claim that the North won the Civil War.

I am baffled how people like that can have a clear conscience when they say things like, "Land of the free, home of the brave". You're absolutely right. Land of the free . . . . As long as you're not a Bosnian, Chinese, Jewish, Hispanic, Native American, or black person. That's not to say that you can't be proud of your Southern heritage. That's fine. Being proud of being from the South is a lot like being proud of your black heritage, if you happen to be African-American.

Another common ridiculous misconception is that "foreigners don't belong in the U.S.". That just screams ignorance. If you're one of the people out there perpetuating that idea, you need to read an American history book. If you do, you might discover that America was founded by nothing but immigrants. The only people that can honestly say they are from this country are Native American. If all of the foreigners were to leave the U.S., the Native Americans would be the only ones left, and we would only have 1.5 million of the approximate 300 million men and women that presently make up the population of the United States. The truth about slavery is enough to make you vomit. You see, historically, only 5% of African slavery was in the U.S. The majority of African slaves were sent to islands in the Caribbean and Brazil. When I learned about slavery in American history as a child, it was very generic and vague, and I'm sure that's probably for a good reason. We can't have kids growing up traumatized. The developmental stages through a child's life shape who the person is going to be as an adult. Showing a child horrifying images and telling them the disturbing truth about the world can have some negative psychological results.

Let me give you some examples of a few horrifying facts about slavery in the U.S.

1. Do you remember that 5% of the African slaves that came to the U.S. that I mentioned before? I didn't say the 5% was a small number. It is estimated that between 700,000—800,000 African slaves inhabited early English America.
2. At the time that slavery was abolished, in the mid-1850s, there were approximately 4,000,000 slaves working in the U.S. Many of them working under intolerable conditions on the larger plantations.
3. Slaves in America were brutally killed without question for something as small as suspicion of theft. In today's world that would be the same as a cop pulling you over and shooting you dead for suspicion of stealing his doughnuts.

Let's focus in on the important factors of slavery for one second. People, who were originally free, were taken from their homes and in many cases their families. They were stripped of all of their belongings, including their freedom; and then made to work against their will, under intolerable conditions, until they were dead. That almost makes me embarrassed to be an American. The fact that our country was founded on principles such as "All men are created equal", is insulting when I think about the fact that, all the while, the U.S. was committing a crime as insulting and degrading as slavery. The way the founding fathers got around it was a technicality. At the time, slaves weren't considered "men"; they were considered property. Because they had no legal rights and were defined as apparently not even being human, slavery was treated with no discourse.

It is, however, an important part of American history. After all, we, as humans, grow through our experiences. It's how we learn. I suppose all we can do now is make sure to never let an act like slavery happen again. That's our responsibility. While we're on the idea of "all men are created equal", am I alone in thinking it was kind of hypocritical of our founding fathers to put THAT statement in writing. While you think about that, I'll let you get a more defined image of what slavery must have been like in America with this next poem.

Shackled Hands

Bearing the weight of shackled hands and feet
This free soul now moved as concrete
The acts of the empowered were inhumane and cruel
Their actions were the fire; their arrogance was the fuel
There were torn bodies in the fields for hours with no end
Under fear of the oppressing whip cracking once again
Yet even under oppression they still retained their pride
A display of perseverance that anyone could stand beside
No matter the struggle, hope remained their inclination
Years of fighting through meaningless litigation
Thankful for all and thankful to be alive
Even though what they had was more than deprived
Taking freedom from anyone is stealing the dark from the night
Because freedom is the right to breathe and every human's right

America wasn't the first country to use slavery, by the way. In fact, it was one of the last. And by the way, a little fact many are unaware of, Africans were in charge of the Trans-Atlantic Slave Trade. Not Americans. Not Caucasians. Africans. I just want to make that part clear. Something else a great many are unaware of, slavery has been around for thousands of years. By the time that the African Slave Trade (Trans-Atlantic Slave Trade) came to America, the majority of the world had already done away with taking part in slavery. Also, in case you unaware, the African Slave Trade didn't conduct business in only North and South America either.

Here's another chunk of history that most people negate. As much as 17 million slaves were sold and shipped to countries all throughout Europe and Asia in the Arab s lave trade.

One of the most overlooked countries that practiced slavery was Sparta. Everyone has this image of Spartan men as the ultimate pugnacious soldiers, sculpted from iron that practiced their combative training every day. As I briefly mentioned in the beginning of this book, the Spartans were able to mold their military the way they did because all of the slaves were busy handling all the regular day-to-day bullshit that the soldiers couldn't be bothered with.

When I say that the slaves handled the day-to-day bullshit, I do mean all of the bullshit, including: pottery, blacksmithing, carpentry, tailoring, farming, sleeping with the wives of the Spartan men while they were away at war. Oh yeah. Make no mistake. In fact, you should look it up. You might be surprised with the results. Why else do you think all of the Spartan soldiers were always in a hurry to get back home during the war Spartan men loved war, but they also loved their women (whenever the men weren't using each other as sexual play toys that is). To the lonely Spartan women that were left waiting for months or years on end for their husbands to return, that average household slave was like a Guatemalan gardener to one of the *Desperate House Wives*. Not that I watch *Desperate House Wives*. I don't want you guys thinking that. I think I'm quickly moving farther and farther away from my original point somehow. Anyway, people have no problem glorifying the idea of soldiers and war. They hate anyone who's not patriotic to their country, but they have no problem with forgetting to mention the thousands of men that were taken and forced to work against their will.

We shouldn't have to pretend for one minute that slavery didn't happen in America. However, we should also learn from our mistakes and ensure that our children do not suffer the same fate.

The moral of this story: Remember the past. Look toward a brighter future. A future that doesn't make any of the same mistakes as we made.

CHAPTER 9

Around Every Corner

April 9th, 2012

I had a brief encounter with racism yesterday. I had to pick up my oldest daughter Serenity and her older sister Elizabeth my ex-wife's other daughter, early from school at about noon. After picking the girls up from school, I had to hurry and drop Myra, my youngest little girl off with her mom.

I decided it would be nice to take Serenity and Elizabeth out for a nice sit down lunch, seeing how I didn't get to do that very often. We arrived at the restaurant and ordered our food. Unfortunately, at the end of my quality father/daughter lunch, I came extremely close to being forced to call my ex-wife Mary to come get the girls for me because I was almost certain I was going to jail that day.

We all ate our food and had fun at lunch. There was only about four or five other customers in the restaurant the whole span of the one hour period that we were there. Here's where the story gets bad. After we were done eating, all three of us got up to pay and leave. While I was standing at the counter paying the bill, a middle-aged, white guy decided to begin saying some very disturbing racist remarks about a black woman on the news. Not only was he making very offensive comments, he was speaking them so loudly that I could have heard them clearly if I was sitting at a table 15 feet away.

I'm someone who abhors racism, or any form of prejudice, really. But I'm also a realist. I know that racism and prejudice are among us at all times, everywhere in the world. I deal with it every day. That doesn't mean that I want my daughters subjected to it if they do not have to be. And forgive me, but it was a little more than difficult for me to not get pissed off when I heard this man say, "Man, look at this shit! This is just another classic example of some black, nigger bitch trying to get away with something that she shouldn't.

When I heard him say that, I had half-a-mind to grab him by the back of his head and slam his face into the marble counter. Maybe after he swallowed some of his own teeth, he would think twice before making another comment like that in front of my two little girls. But again, acting like that in front of my daughter and her sister would probably scar my little girls more than they already were from his loud, obscene remarks. It took some strong resilience, but I was able to refrain from turning his face into a batch of runny eggs. I still maintain that it was my respect for my girls that got me through that day without going to jail for assault and battery.

Now, some of you may be saying to yourselves, "Come on, that's not that bad". Like I said before, I'm aware that racism is everywhere. We can't escape it. It's as inevitable as Agent Smith fighting Neo in *The Matrix*. It still doesn't make it right. This man forced me to explain something to my 8 year old daughter and her 11 year old sister that I was not mentally or emotionally prepared for. I had to tell them what the man at the restaurant said, why it is wrong to ever say it, and why I never wanted either of them to repeat anything he said ever again.

Children are not stupid; they are incredibly impressionable. In no way, shape, or form do I want my daughters growing up naïve or ignorant of the ways of the world because I kept them sheltered. That being said, I would rather do it at the appropriate time, setting, and age that I see fit, and not because some dumb, ignorant, waste-of-his-father's-sperm decided to choose for me.

Moral of this story: You can say whatever you want to me. But if you do it in front of my children, I'm inclined to chop your balls off. Actually, I guess that's more of a warning rather than a moral.

CHAPTER 10

I Didn't Know God Hated Gays?

There are so many jokes running through my head right now that I can't even begin to separate them. I will be addressing male homosexuals primarily, as apparently everyone in society is totally OK with a female being gay as long as they get to watch. I call that pretty hypocritical of men and women both. I'm not saying I don't knock my junk around to the thought of a little girl on girl action, because I do, in great frequency I might add. The difference is that I don't persecute gay men either. I think two dudes gettin' it on is disgusting, but it's just who they are. Let's start with some of the common idioms associated with homosexuals. Such as . . .

Homo
Gay
Fag
Faggot
Fanny-Bandit
Butt-Pirate
Ass-Jockey
Fudge-Packer
Cock-Sucker and
Pole-Smoker

I'm going to be honest with you. I have no idea if any of those terms were supposed to be hyphenated; it just looked better that way. I'm sure there are several more common terms out there but I'm just going to stop there.

One of the worst forms of prejudice is people hating gays for being gay; even though a gay person's sexual preference has no impact on someone else' life. No matter what the cause of homosexual behavior is, the persecution of someone for their individual sexual preference is wrong. Now it goes without saying that your individual personality may be uncomfortable with homosexuals, and that is also not something that you can control. But being uncomfortable and going out and rallying or maliciously beating a gay person for no reason, are two completely different things. If you want to hate me or call me weak for saying that, fine. I'm not going to lose any sleep over it, and I don't think anyone else will either.

In that same sense, if a homosexual person knows you are not gay and still tries to come on to you persistently, they too have crossed the same line. But in that situation, they are not wrong for being gay but for the same reason it's wrong to come on to a heterosexual person that doesn't want you to. It's just impersonal. Making someone feel uncomfortable just to make you feel good is selfish and hurtful. Furthermore, I think someone that does that needs to take a good look in the mirror. How would you feel if someone else did that to you? Try that the next time someone has a different opinion than you. Put the shoe on the other foot before you speak or act. You might be able to save yourself some jail time.

From a sociological perspective, a gay person is simply different from what society deems normal. Society doesn't understand it. Gay-haters don't understand what a man could possibly find attractive about a penis. Honestly, I don't understand what it is about the male penis that women find attractive. That could just be because I have such an unattractive penis, but who knows. The first natural response when you don't understand something is to separate yourself from it out of fear and then proceed to full-on hatred. All that does is breed a society of intolerance and prejudice for something the homosexual community has no control over.

Yes, I do believe that homosexuality is a biological factor, far more than a personal choice or an environmentally related matter. However, I am not discussing what the cause is. I am discussing why it is wrong to hate the whole gay community just for being different. It doesn't matter why they are different; they are not you. You wouldn't hate people who prefer lamb chops just because you happen to prefer cheeseburgers would you?

Now, you know I can't talk about people hating gays and not mention Christian extremists. It literally disgusts me to the point of vomiting to see that guy with a tattoo of "Only God can judge me" at a Christian rally picketing against gays. And I swear, if one more person tries to tell me that homosexuality is wrong because God says it's an abomination, I'm just going to pack up and freakin' move to Timbuk Fuck. I am so sick of hearing "Leviticus 18:22" and "Leviticus 20:13". Yeah, I get it. Your God hates gays. And let's evaluate that particular verse for a second.

> Leviticus 20:13
> "If a man also lie with mankind, as he lieth with a woman, both of them have committed an abomination: they shall surely be put to death; their blood shall be upon them."

Their blood shall be upon them???? They had gay sex. They didn't commit armed robbery and rape young women. My, what an inspiring example of peace and tranquility from a fair and just God. I noticed that there was no mention of women lying with women. I guess God says it's OK to be a lesbian and act out all of the fantasies that I have been jerking off to over the last couple of decades, but it's not OK to be a gay man. That is bold faced hypocrisy. And yes, before you send me all of your hate mail, I would say the same thing to anyone guilty of persecuting others for their beliefs or life choices. It is none of my business what a gay man or woman does in the privacy of their own home, as long as they show me the same respect that I show them. It's not like I have to watch a gay guy live out his sodomizing dreams.

Violent acts against homosexual men are growing at such a fast pace that soon they will outnumber racial hate crimes. Listen to this monstrous tale of douche-bag conviction:

March 14, 2007, in Florida, a 25-year-old homosexual male named Ryan Skipper was found dead after being stabbed 20 times and having his throat slit. When asked why they attacked Mr. Skipper, the two alleged murderers, William David Brown, Jr. and Joseph Eli Bearden had this to say, "He was a faggot".

So, if you're standing beside me and help kick the shit out of a bunch of ninjas that show up to kill me, and then you go home to give your boyfriend, err . . . lover . . . err . . . . whatever-the-hell they call it, the "Dirty Sanchez", you're OK in my book. You had my back, and you didn't try to make me feel uncomfortable by asking if you can rub my shoulders and force me to watch the *Twilight* movies with you. That's all I ask. That's the way I look at it. For you, it may not be so black and white. I have my own opinion that I am entitled to. It's only fair then, if I'm entitled to my own opinion, people are justifiably entitled to their own stupidity too . . . . **OPINION!!!!** I meant to say opinion.

Very few gay men and women will try to make a pass at a friend of theirs that is a heterosexual and of the same gender. Is it full-proof? No. Of course not. You're always going to have the occasional weirdo that you hear about on TV that serves as the reason for a lot of the misconception about homosexuals. When I hear or read about these stories I always go straight to the scene from *Silence of the Lambs* when "Buffalo Bill" (who is played by Ted Levine) does that wiener tuck thing and dances in front of the mirror. That shit is disturbing.

It's extreme cases like that which are probably the reason for the perpetuation of the typical homosexual male residing within the gay community. That kind of wackjob is an extremely rare case and is severely deranged in the head. He was probably forced to wear dresses and play with dolls as a child and grew into the gender-confused, throwing-people-into-a-20 ft. well inside of his basement kind of murderer that frightens the majority of society, me included. Somehow, I can see the gay men of the world looking at someone like that and being like, "Seriously dude? You're starting to freak **ME** out." That sounds pretty bad coming from somebody who uses another man's penis as a way in which to apply lip-gloss.

Moral of the story: What one person does in the privacy of their own home has no bearing on you, unless they're keeping you held captive in the privacy of their own home. If that's the case, you should call Jodie Foster to flush the criminal weirdo out of hiding.

CHAPTER 11

The American Misogynist

Being someone who has written too many sappy songs and love poetry to women in the past, I have learned a thing or two about what constitutes genuine, chivalrous actions vs. romantic gestures that are stemmed completely from the thought of getting a woman to take her clothes off. Women are from Venus. Men are from Mars. Men are simple. Women are complicated. etc. etc. Blah, blah, blah.

When I write sappy poetry it's usually written with a deep sense of sincerity. It's still sappy, and I usually have hopes of using the poetry to not only touch a woman's heart but also her vagina. I'm sure that's not easy to hear, and I probably shouldn't say that knowing, at some point, a woman is going to read this. Making a statement like that could very well ruin my chances of meeting any women that are game for using my dick as a flute. Speaking of sappy poetry, take these poems that I wrote for women in the past.

Is This Real?

How could this be possible?
I thought I had forgotten how to feel
My love for you that burns within
Is now the only thing that is real
I cannot taste the freshest fruit
Nor smell the sweetest rose
My sense of direction has faded away
But I can follow my heart wherever it goes
I see your face in every page
Of every book that I read
You are not something I can do without
You are now everything that I need
You are the bird on the window
You are everything I have seen
I am a king that can not see past his nose
If I am not standing by my queen

Your Touch

Alone at night I sit and I think
How I long to see your face
And indulge in you the sweetest drink
From your lips comes the sweetest taste
I speak to you in simple words
Soft and serene, I whisper sweetly
But my softness bears not how my heart burns
I dare not confess my love discretely
I would sing of my love into the skies
For any soul that would hear my song
And for any that would tell me otherwise
I would laugh and say they are wrong
I know in my mind and my heart what is real
I have found what I was searching to find
Your touch is what every man desires to feel
And I am proud to call you mine

In this section of the book I will discuss many of the areas that surround these typified arguments and exactly how they correlate with gender persecution of the past and present and how society has evolved.

First of all, there is a very clear line between chivalry and respect. Yes, women are fragile creatures capable of crippling a man emotionally, controlling the quality and quantity of sex between a couple, and winning the majority of spouse abuse and child support and custody cases throughout recent history. But why do you suppose that is, exactly? If we're talking about women being treated with equal rights and privileges, there is not much equal to the aforementioned topics is there? Perhaps we can look at things historically to find some answers.

Historically women were given no rights to speak among men. They had no right to vote, organize, be involved in politics and in many cases defy their husbands' final word. Sounds like a pretty cruel and unjust world we lived in doesn't it? Do you know why? Because those are cruel and unjust actions of persecution against women. That's not to say that the topics discussed in the paragraph above are not completely relevant of today's western society. It merely explains perhaps why we are at the place that we are with women's rights and women's place in society.

Women weren't allowed to make changes to religious texts, even if they were accurate. An interesting point when you think of female figures such as Mary, the mother of Jesus of Nazareth and Mary Magdalene whom may have had something important to add. During the Salem Witch Trials women were drowned for heresy and alleged witchcraft. How many women were brutally and mercilessly killed and cast into the depths of Hell? Henry VIII had no problem killing his wives when it meant he could get a new wife and attempt to distract his countrymen from the dire need of economical restoration and general hardships of their day to day lives. But how many queens have ever executed the king of a country? Intriguing?

Women in Politics: I can't count how many times I have heard old-fashioned (well pretty much old in general) people tell me that women don't belong in politics. Most notably, a woman should never be allowed to reside as president of the United States. I hope for the sake of humanity I don't need to recite certain lines from the Declaration of Independence again.

Usually it's the ridiculous notion that women shouldn't be allowed into office because they menstruate and with menstruation comes the dreaded, life-sucking demon known as PMS. You don't have to be a feminist to think that is completely ridiculous. I have been married twice and in a few other relationships that I know of, and I can tell you personally, I've had more mood swings than the majority of the women I have been with. And as far as I am aware, I have never had a period. Medically speaking, we can't overlook the fact that women experience heightened emotional complexities during these periods. But I hardly see how it cannot be considered hypocritical to say women don't belong in politics because of that and then turn around and speak of women as gentle, fragile, and harmless beings. Yes, it's true. They generally oppose war more than most men. So do a lot of Democrats. But that's not to say that there aren't the occasional females out there that would cease to live if they didn't have someone reminding them to keep breathing every few seconds.

Women in the Military: There's no women allowed in combat arms. And do you want to know why? All right; I'll tell you. It must be because of the immense trauma that men would face at the sight of . . . . A tampon? . . . . Well then you tell me, because if that's not it, then I have no fucking clue what it is. Clearly, it must be because women on a submarine would distract the men on the sub from keeping up with all of their typical male butt-sex. And, I guess, that's just not something that the Navy is willing to give up. On a serious note, on April 29th, 2010, the Department of the Navy formally announced that women were permitted to serve onboard submarines, an opportunity that was denied until that point. Hopefully, the future of women in the military and workplace will have equal treatment on every plane, assuming that's what they really want.

Women in the Workplace: Recently, women have begun dominating not only the administrative careers fields, but also the more male-oriented trades such as carpentry, drafting, welding . . . . The list is pretty long, but I think you see where I'm going with this. A few years back, when I was doing commercial carpentry, there was a woman that could go heels with any male carpenter on the job. Granted, I think she had a bigger penis than me, based on her muscles and tattoos, but she was a woman none-the-less. At least I think she was? Maybe she was between stages of the gender transformation operation? Anyway . . .

I think one of the main reasons that marriage and the divorce rate have changed over the last 25 years, is also probably due to the popularity of women in the workplace. Up until the mid-to-late 1900s, woman's place in America was in the home. Women were responsible for taking care of the children, cooking, cleaning, etc.

Women used to be reliant upon men for their economic survival as well as the continuity of a normal family. Today, things are different; women can survive without men. Women are working during the day, going to college at night, taking their kids to soccer practice, and still finding time to hit the gym just before they make a friendly "booty call" to come over to take advantage of them. Women don't rely on men the way they used to. Hell, while I was laid off from my job as a carpenter, my wife at the time supported our family, off and on, for two years.

Lately, I feel like women are taking hold of the wheel and knocking men off the racetrack completely. And you know what? That's fine. If men don't want to be pushed aside, maybe men should step up, start getting educated and give women a run for their money. It's a brand new world guys. You might want to wake up and start paying attention.

The moral of this story: Ladies, you've been waiting for equal rights for a long time. Don't ruin it for the future generations of women by (if you'll excuse the pun) screwing it up the first chance you are given.

CHAPTER 12

Think Before You Speak

A friend of mine used to say, "Tact is for people who aren't smart enough to be sarcastic". Thank God that guy isn't in the human resources field. It made me laugh, but usually anything that makes you laugh like that is probably not politically correct. Political correctness aside, the only thing that is accomplished when someone uses a derogatory slur is the excessive demonstration of their ignorance, publicly to everyone around them.

I'll admit it's rather funny in a cavalier setting to hear comedians drop the "N-Word", but it is still hypocritical. Racial and derogatory slurs are wrong regardless of who is saying them.

To the African-Americans out their listening, I hope you can hear me. It is completely hypocritical to use a racial slur in casual conversation and then be ready to spend life in prison for murder if a person from another race uses the same term. It's also unfair to try to use an excuse like, "The context of the word is changed when black people use it." No, it isn't. The rules don't change just because it suits you. White people if you are applauding right now, STOP IT! Stop calling black people racial slurs.

I don't care if you don't mean any harm when you say it, most of the time you do anyway. But even if you don't mean any harm, all you are doing is giving fuel to the fire that is racism. You give African-Americans another reason to think that every white person hates them, and I for one do not want to be associated with that.

Another excuse that is absolutely ridiculous is the recently common, "Oh, its cool. One of my friends is black", in reference to when a white person wants to call a black person "Nigga". That is one of the dumbest things I have ever heard. And believe me; I have heard a lot of dumb statements in my short-lived time on Earth. I apologize for not being able to find a better synonymous word for dumb, but that's probably the best way to describe it.

Yes, I am sure the entire black community will completely accept you calling them the most hated word they have because you just so happen to have one black friend who says it's OK. Are you an idiot? I know I don't want some white moron telling African-Americans that it's OK to call him "cracker" because that is the same as saying it's fine to call all white people by that term. It's not; it's not OK at all. When are people going to wake up and see that there is no reason to create a system of labeling for different races? We are all the same. That's why there is no need to label people.

I remember one time in particular, while I was working as a correctional officer; I was walking one of the wings of the building, checking on the inmates, and out of nowhere, one of them yelled out, "Yeah, you better keep walking, honky". At first, I was pissed off and I wanted to find out who it was. As I started to turn around, I remember thinking to myself, "Wait a minute. This guy just called me 'Honky'. This ain't the fuckin' *Jeffersons*". My anger and frustration quickly turned to sorrow when I realized that this guy has been locked up for so long that he had no idea that white people weren't called that anymore. Suddenly, the use of his racial slur, however outdated it was, didn't bother me so much, and my life didn't seem so bad.

America has grown in terms of civility, tolerance, and understanding. I am obviously not saying the U.S is anywhere near where I would like our country to be, but we have definitely come a long way. For instance, in the year 2008, Barack Obama was elected president of the United States, effectively making him the first African-American president. I think we're all aware the white supremacists in America are ready to blow their own brains out over having a black U.S. president. And I would probably be lying if I said that I would cry a lot of tears over their racist corpses. Sarcasm aside, I honestly don't feel suicide is a healthy end to anyone's life, and I can't have anyone thinking that I want anyone dead just for stating what they think. Again, it's the actions of people that I place in check. If we can at least start with that, then maybe we can begin to positively affect the psyche of racism.

Now that I have said how important the ethnic and cultural growth of our country is, it's time to touch on a serious problem. It appears some African-Americans seem to be having difficulty letting go of the past and feel the need to seek hatred toward today's Caucasian Americans. I am sorry if my white ancestors owned black slaves. That does not mean that I ever discriminated, hated, or oppressed so much as one black person. Therefore, if you are an African-American that is seeking justice because, "White people today owe black people for 200 years of slavery", you're living a lie.

I'm sorry if that offends anyone, but that is not justice; that is revenge and there is a difference. I am a huge admirer of Dr. Martin Luther King Jr. because he was such an important influence in the Civil Rights Movement. Civil Rights are about the freedoms that every man and woman should be given. Dr. King stood for equality and acceptance. Those are ideas to be admired, not smeared. His murder was a tragedy. America lost an icon of equality when he died. But years later his death has been used in propaganda and speeches to smear his original message to actually begin perpetuating the opposite of what he fought for so long to achieve.

Real quick, I have to say something that has been on my mind, even though it is seemingly not as pertinent as the rest of this chapter. I am so sick of hearing white people saying, "How come black people get black history month? How come black people have black TV shows and black movies?" I am going to tell the you why. Because white people have everything else! Oh my God! I have never heard such a whiny bunch of bullshit in my life.

Let's get real, people. There is nothing wrong with black people wanting to celebrate their heritage or their growth in America. So they make black TV shows and black movies. Guess what? White people have been doing that for years. And frankly, "White Entertainment" severely outnumbers "Black Entertainment". The Caucasian population just chooses not to call it white.

The other annoying one I am getting tired of is, "The token black guy is in every white movie and TV show just to keep the production company from getting sued." Yes, there are certain minority numbers that have to be met in order to avoid litigation processes. I don't care if it is true. Perhaps the casting crew should have put more than one black person in the program or film. Or maybe, and I know this sounds crazy, but maybe the actors and actresses that are cast for the roles on TV and films should be hired based on their acting abilities.

It's true a black man can't fill the role of a white character if the fact that the character is white is paramount to the story. But ask yourself this: How many roles are versatile among races? Probably a lot more than those that aren't. So to White America, I have a small request. Get over it people. It's no big deal. I mean goddamn, you already have everything else. I think you can pretty much still call that a win if you happen to think African-Americans and Caucasians are in a competition.

I come across people all the time that immediately jump to asking, "Well, what if someone calls you a racial slur first?" To which I usually reply with a question of my own such as, "Do you really want to appear just as ignorant as the person you are talking about?"

There are also a lot of times that I also like to use statements such as, "Oh, I'm sorry. I didn't realize you were 10 years old". Granted, that comes off as a little more sarcastic. None the less, rhetorical statements like that can be a very useful tool when attempting to demonstrate a point to someone who is acting irrationally or hurtful.

I don't want to make this whole section about just black vs. white slurs though. So let's look at some of the most prevalent derogatory slurs that are out there in the world being abused daily. Things like:

Origin of Derogatory Slur	Actual Derogatory Slur
Chinks	Chinese
Gooks	Korean
Towel-Heads/Rag-Heads	Middle Eastern
Crauts	German
Faggots/Fags	Homosexuals
W.O.P. (With Out Papers)	Italian
Spics/Wetbacks	Mexican
Frogs	French

Sadly, this is only a small percentage of the ongoing list that is improperly used. The misuses of words like these aren't just common among the ignorant and prejudiced people of the world either. The U.S. military, for example, even uses derogatory labeling as a means to win wars. During the Korean War, the military began using the racial slur "Slant Eyes" and "Gooks". In Vietnam, the U.S. used the term "Charlie" in correlation to the phonetic letter C, which when spoken, is pronounced "Charlie". The C was in representation of the "C" in the word "Cong", as in, the Viet Cong.

From Desert Storm, all the way through the wars in Iraq and Afghanistan, the U.S. military has brought the term "Rag Head" or "Towel Head" into popular circulation. The U.S. military uses this form of indoctrination to instill a blind prejudice into the men and women serving our country proudly. The prejudice happens without being noticed by brainwashing the American military during their initial phases of training. The prejudice makes each soldier a more effective killing machine by creating the mentality that as a soldier, you are not killing real people; you are killing an idea.

The idea that the soldiers are killing is that every citizen of humanity that stands against the U.S. needs to die. By doing this, the country's soldiers don't hesitate to pull the trigger. I understand why the military would see this as a positive way to help win wars. Unfortunately, this type of indoctrination carries with it more than just the zombies in America's military forces. To explain my point, think about every military movie or TV show that Hollywood has ever put out into the mainstream. Hollywood takes the military's views and distributes them to the hundreds of millions of people in the country. How many people that have never served in the military have watched the films *Blackhawk Down, Platoon, Tigerland, We Were Soldiers, Pearl Harbor, The Hurt Locker,* or *Full-Metal Jacket*? All of these men and women in America have Hollywood's perception of the truth, regardless of how much content in the films are accurate. In a way, Hollywood is just as guilty of indoctrinating America as the military is. Hate me if you want to, but it's the truth.

Now for the really bad news, derogatory slurs are different than curse words or swear words. People often tell me that I'm wrong for writing satire and that swearing in my writing is irresponsible. They say that it's unethical, and demonstrates my lack of vocabulary and maturity to the rest of the world. Well, that's fine. They can all go fornicate themselves because they're all just a bunch of fuckheads. I say that because I'm not swearing at any of them, nor am I forcing them to read anything. If you don't like what I have to say, close the book and go do something else. Now I know what you're thinking, but stick with me and I'll explain why.

Censorship falls on the individual, or in the event of a child, the parent. If you discover that the book you're reading has content that you disagree with, the solution is as easy as closing the book. Besides, have you ever read one of those erotica novels? It's like graphic porn. Why don't the people of the world go bother those authors? Tell THEM why THEY'RE wrong and leave ME alone.

Anyway, back to the original argument at hand. Swearing is related more to sociological factors such as geography, language, and education than any other variables. After all, if a Mexican swears at you in Spanish and you have no idea what they said, do you really consider it swearing? There are also other factors that come into play such as tone and the way that the swear word is used that determine its morality. Let's take a look at the idea of interpretation with this example.

Alex P. Hewing is a shithead.
Alex P. Hewing is a craphead.
Alex P. Hewing is a poophead.

All three of these statements are true. I am a shithead. All three of these statements also mean the same thing. The interpretation and understanding of the word determines its morality. If you argue that belief, think about the parents (myself included) that tell their children it's OK to say poop, but it's not OK to say shit, or even crap. The sociological variables such as geography, or the location in which one spends their entire life, carries with it the accepted morality of a word. Let's have some fun with it and add some variables to put it in simplest, understandable terms.

In the town of Podunk
X = a bad word
Y = a word that is not bad

In the town of Timbuk Fuck
Y = a bad word
X = a word that is not bad

In this example, the two towns are completely geographically separated and have never had any interaction with one another. When Bob, who lives in Podunk, finally reaches the town of Timbuk Fuck for the first time and uses "X" which is determined in his geographical location as not being a bad word, the people of Timbuk Fuck may very well attempt disassociation from him without Bob ever knowing why.

There are other reasons for arguing the morality of swearing also. If a person uses a word like bitch, which has more than one meaning, one of which is not to be taken as a swear word, is that considered swearing? But if you don't believe me after hearing that load of crap, think about this. In French, the word "seal" is spelled phoque and pronounced exactly as it looks. On 26 April 1278 John Le Fucker was arrested and imprisoned in England for murder. Even more funny is that in Austria there is a town that is spelled Fucking. I shit you not. Look it up if you don't believe me. God, I would just love to be from there so that when people ask where I'm from, I can be perfectly honest when I tell them "I'm from Fucking, Austria" and know that I'm not swearing. So, the next time someone tells you that swearing is inappropriate in literature, do me a favor (because I'm not there to do it for you), look them square in the face and proudly say, "FUCK YOU!!!!"

Words

Words can leave a scar not visible by the eye
But are worn very heavily on the victim's heart
They can cut deeper than any knife can reach
And the pain can be carried through a lifetime
There is no pain like the pain from words
No man and no woman is born immune to it
It poisons the mind to the point of self-hate
And our only defense to shield us from this poison
Is to turn a deaf ear to the person who speaks it
Day after day lives are wasted away
All for the pride of a few simple words

I don't care how you try to rationalize it. It's wrong to use derogatory words when generalizing a whole group. On the contrary argument however, I also can't help but feel that in today's world, the term "politically correct" gets taken a step (or twelve) too far. 50 years ago, it was perfectly fine to call men and women in prison, inmates. Today, correctional officers at an adult institution of corrections are told to refer to them as offenders. My God, by tomorrow, we'll all be calling them guests at a resort.

The moral of the story: Wouldn't it just be easier to call everyone by their names?

CHAPTER 13

Dems vs. Reps

I don't know how many times someone has told me they were a democrat or a republican because that's what their parents were and they don't know any better. This is right up there with the whole staying in the same religion as your family because that's how you were raised.

If you want to cook a turkey the same way your mom taught you, that's fine. I don't even care if you want to adopt the family practices of taking the kids out for ice cream on Sundays. Hey, more power to you. But electing to never even accept the possibility of choosing a different political party just because you don't want to upset or disappoint your parents is ludicrous. While you're at it why don't you go ahead and where a shirt that says "YES, I AM AN ADULT WHO HAS NO POWER TO CHOOSE ANYTHING FOR MYSELF", or perhaps "I STILL DO WHATEVER MY PARENTS TELL ME TO DO EVEN THOUGH MY OWN KIDS ARE ALMOST OUT OF SCHOOL". It's true that last one would be difficult to fit on a shirt, but my sarcasm isn't bound by physical limitations like that.

I'm not sure what's more disturbing—believing whatever your family believes with no opinion for yourself, or not actually seeing anything wrong with doing that. Yet it happens all time. I've seen it countless times. I'm not going to sit here and argue which political party is right because we all know that's a matter of perception and opinion. Let me run that by you again. Political stance is a matter of opinion. So please, by all means, have one. Stop letting other people make your decisions for you. Think about it. What's to say the person whose beliefs you are adopting aren't originating from another moron who inherited their beliefs from the very first generation of morons.

There could potentially be a hundred years long daisy chain of ignorant people passing on their stupidity to others. It's probably a good idea for me to note that I firmly believe that **politics = corruption**, one way or another. I truly think that in order to be successful and advance in politics you almost have to be corruptible. I didn't say to be in politics. I said to be successful in politics, meaning you can probably get into a political office and still maintain your integrity and veracity without fault. I bring this point to light because my political stance is independent due to said belief.

There are other variables that encourage such strong convictions about something as important as a political stance. For example, I don't believe that U.S. presidential elections are legitimately organized because regardless of the number of votes that are accrued, it is ultimately decided upon by the Electoral College; a fact that far too many voters are unaware of.

Our founding fathers thought it would serve as a fail-safe if our country's government should literally fall victim to anarchy. In my opinion, if George Washington and Thomas Jefferson wanted the decision making power of presidential elections to be in the hands of the Electoral College, they should be the only ones that even gets to vote. Yes, I am aware that the Electoral College is designed to act on the behalf of the constituents they individually represent. But it's still not right.

If you're wondering if I myself am an anarchist, the answer is no. But let the record state that I don't think there is anything wrong with anarchists. Anarchists are one of those misunderstood groups among the general population that have been labeled with a negative stereotype as disturbers of the peace and harmony of organized government. That generality is partially accurate. However, the overemphasized actions of true anarchists are far from the label they have been stuck living with.

I challenge anyone to educate themselves on what actually constitutes an anarchist. After reading it, if you still feel so negative about anarchists or genuinely still believe they are completely wrong for their beliefs, I would at least have the satisfaction of knowing you educated yourself before making your final decision. I can respect that. Getting back to the political argument at hand; it's just another form of improper indoctrination. I think I need another Xanax. So while I'm going to get that, why don't you read up on a few of my thoughts on politics?

A Free Man

You will never see a more proud fool
Than the man and woman to your left and right
Used so well like hardened tools
And so content with their own plight
Oblivious to the changes that would better their dreams
As if they were a blind man watching TV
And only possess the freedom of a puppet on a string
That can be tossed aside so easily
You will never see a truly free man
Ever ask for the permission to think
Or speak his mind with fear of reprimand
Because his freedom is a ship that will never sink
There are those among us who are battered and bruised
By the bureaucratic whips that crash upon us like waves
But a man that chooses not to choose
Has unknowingly already made himself a slave

There is no right or wrong when deciding which political party is better. If the political parties are corrupted by their representation from the inside, then the organization is corrupted.

> **"A poisoned red apple is just as dangerous as a poisoned green apple."**

-Alex P. Hewing

I have my own opinion of former president William Jefferson Clinton's political choices while in office. Regardless of his actions politically, the reason people focus so much on his discrete sexual encounters outside of his marriage (i.e. Tagging the very unattractive Monica Lewinsky) is because any sort of immoral weakness or vulnerability found in the most powerful man in the country, represents weakness or vulnerability in our country's government. It doesn't matter how many other people in America would have done or have done the same thing. What matters is that he is representing our country. On a side note, don't you think Clinton should have renamed his private quarters the "**Oral Office**" after that whole mess?

The truth is, our government has consistently gone back and forth from democratic to republican over and over again usually about every eight years. If the country is under democratic rule, by the end of those eight years the country is tired of being run by corrupt democrats who make promises they never keep. So America decides, "Yeah, it's time to put this country back under republicans who can straighten everything out". So when election time comes, we switch back to Right-Wing hypocritical politicians who make promises they never keep.

The Political Realignment was a huge turning point in American history that political science majors love to do their thesis on. But in reality it didn't matter. The Republican Party basically became the Democratic Party during the shift. Try looking at it this way: If both parties were corrupt before The Realignment, and today they're still corrupt, what has changed?

Uneducated, undecided voters make me sad. Usually because they have no background on the person they are voting for. If this is an example of you, I'm sorry. If you are casting your vote based on strictly your political preference, or worse, whatever the general population is going with, I only have one thing to say. Way to go, Social Conformity!

I know I have never voted, but if I was to ever vote, it would be extremely well researched and would be my decision. I wouldn't let other people sway my decision based on popularity. You'll have to excuse me; I'm not in high school. I place my decisions based on the issues the individual political candidate relates the most logically to my own ideas and the ideas that I believe will be best for the country.

That's another problem. A lot of people place their vote on whichever candidate can put the most money in their wallet. That choice has less to do with the benefit of the country and more to do with self-gratification. And for all of the Democrats cheering after reading that, that's not an attack on Republicans. Democrats elect who will put the most money in their wallets also. Although, I'll admit it makes more sense than voting for someone you know absolutely nothing about.

There are people that cast their votes at the booth without any knowledge of the person they are voting for. If you are someone that claims you honestly believe your vote counts, why would you ever vote for someone that may not share one belief or idea in common with you? Next time, if you want to choose who to vote for and not feel guilty for not knowing anything, just flip a coin. You'll probably get the same results.

Moral of the Story: It doesn't matter if you're left wing or right wing, as long as the person to your left and right vote the same as you. Man, we live in a perfect world.

Chapter 14

The Education Curve

Note from the Author:
Ignorance is the poison that doesn't show up on a toxicology analysis.

How much farther could you go in life if you had more education? Don't bother thinking about it. It was a rhetorical question. The actual answer is: You are limitless.

I asked a guy from work the other day about basic questions in American history. He couldn't answer any of them. I asked an American adult some grade school and maybe high school level questions and he couldn't answer them. How is any American supposed to take pride in that? This is why India is ranked #1 in the world academically, and the U.S. is ranked . . . . SHIT. Americans have been so busy making fun of Indians for having dots on their foreheads that we neglected to notice we have fallen down the educational ladder, far below other countries.

On that note, if you're not one of the people that enjoy studying the sciences or history, you could spend your time, money, and effort educating yourself in the arts. You could try learning a foreign language, how to play a new instrument, painting, writing, sculpting, or drawing. I'm not saying; I'm just saying. While I'm calming down . . . Here, enjoy these poems about not contributing to society's growing norm of a lethargic, uneducated America.

<u>Why Wait?</u>

Now is the time to take the lead
Do not procrastinate, instead find the drive
It is far too easy to watch the world pass
Rather than turn the gears that bring life to our lives
It is in our own nature we find pleasure in nothing
As we lie around relaxing and watch others do the same
As opposed to enduring the effort to stand up
And fight this reputation that plagues our name
Sedentary lifestyles bring nothing to your side
Except shame and weakness in this life that moves fast
So I will tell those that would hear me in faith and take head
Start living your lives and get up off your ass

<u>Opened Doors</u>

It is through education that we find
Opened doors to whole new worlds
Filled with the treasures that cannot be found
Among any tomb or the bottom of any ocean
It is in words where we lose ourselves
And begin a greater journey than any man
And in great equations unsolved by others
That can truly offer a greater challenge than any foe
In novels we find ourselves lost for days
Carefully awaiting the turn of the next page
And in science we can unlock the marvels of life
And record them in our history books for all time
In languages we have learned to reach out to others
And share what we have learned with the other tongues of the world

One of my favorite quotes that honestly can come off a bit on the misleading side, comes from one of the United States' very own founding fathers, Mr. Benjamin Franklin who said, "He who teaches himself hath a fool for a master". I say that quote is misleading because what it is meant to imply versus its very literal meaning are two completely different things that can be easily misinterpreted.

I teach myself things all the time, and I also encourage people to study and learn things on their own. However, as with any subject you are learning about, make sure you are learning correctly. Read up, study, and learn from a variety of sources if at all possible in order to achieve the best overall consensus on the matter. After all, a republican and democrat with political science degrees are both very knowledgeable in the areas of politics, but they will have extremely different views of what is correct or accurate. Even if you have a teacher, if the teacher is wrong, then you will learn wrong. Remember, practice doesn't make perfect. Perfect practice makes perfect.

Somebody once asked me what the proper education is. In my opinion, everything is, in moderation at least. I think it's important to know a little bit about everything. I think education, as a whole, is one of the most paramount tools mankind has ever accomplished, and it's the absolute best tool of trade when standing against ignorance. Obviously, everyone has certain areas that fascinate them more than others. Likewise, they may have an area that they learn more easily.

For me, math was always my Achilles Heel. When I started college, I had to take my math placement test to see where I should begin my studies. For anyone out there who doesn't know how college classes are categorized and labeled, no college class can ever come before 101. You know, Psychology 101, Geography 101, that sort of thing. You can imagine how I felt when I found out that, according to my math score, I had to start my math studies at Math 001.

I know what you're thinking; I put the 1 and the 0 in the wrong spots. No. No, I didn't unfortunately. I had to take three semesters of math, just so I could get to a 100 level math class, which is considered college freshman math. The reason being, the first three math classes, Math 001, 002, and 003 were all remedial. That means not one of the first three math classes transferred when I switched schools, because they weren't considered to be college-level math. Not the coolest thing to have to tell people, but I believe in owning my flaws. It's the only way to grow as a person.

It's easy to see how a question such as "What is the proper education", can be very skewed by everything from matters of opinion, personal interests, and even a person's values. One could argue that if you're passionate about music, then your education should center on music, and that's fine. Just don't forget to educate yourself in other areas. You don't have to be as knowledgeable in other areas as you are in music; it's just a good philosophy in life.

You don't have to be enrolled in college either to continue your education. People tell me all time that they can't afford to go back to school, or they don't have the time. Both of those excuses are bullshit. We live in a world of infinite, educational resources. It's called the Internet. Not to mention the fact that, back in the day, they invented these things called libraries. If you don't enjoy reading books, and you're as poor as I am, most libraries even offer Internet and computers available for you to use, for free.

This is the part of the book where I discuss how everyone can easily study multiple areas without necessarily changing their day to day habits. I truly believe that if you are doing your own studying, the hours you spent trying to get to the top score on the most recent first person shooter, will feel wasted in comparison to the wealth of knowledge that was available all this time. You could very well free yourself from the figurative prison that you've been living in.

First, let's talk about psychology. This field is excellent to study because it has practical use. It's especially good to study if you couple it with the concentration of an area such as criminal justice or criminology. Psychology teaches us about how to live healthier lifestyles, how to cope with addictions; it also offers valuable lessons in relationship counseling and child care. Every parent can appreciate that. I don't know too many decent parents that want their kids growing up unstable, immoral, and ending up in one of the many institutions for adult corrections (A.K.A. prison).

In your leisure of time, you can read up on religion. I hope you do. If you do your own research on religions, and not just your own, you might find you've been spending hours of your life, every week, on something that you don't even believe in. You may come to find out that you have been an Atheist or an Agnostic, all along, and just didn't know it. Who knows? You may even find out that Buddhism is the religion for you.

While researching religion you can begin reading up on history, as history and religion are always interconnected. And not just the history from whatever country you hail from. You can study the history of the U.S., Great Britain, Italy, France, Spain, Macedonia, Israel, Egypt, China, Greece, Mexico, Russia, and all over South America.

Since you're already studying the history of all of these places, do yourself a favor and learn all of their locations on a map. Guess what? Now you can scratch geography off of your to-do list. It amazes me how many adults can't point out some of the most common places on a globe. But why should your education have to stop there?

You're already learning about all of these different countries' locations, and their history. You might as well read up on some of their cultures, and social norms. Chances are if you study the religion, geography, and history of that particular area, you're going to learn a lot of the culture anyway. For those who don't know, that's an area of academics known as social science. It includes areas of study such as anthropology and sociology. Social science is an area that I wish more people would read up on, because it teaches us respect and understanding for other cultures, races, etc. I think that's something the world can always use more of.

If you're a natural science nut, you're in luck because most sciences are connected to one another. If you like staring at the beautiful collection of celestial bodies known as the stars, you can study astronomy. Every year, through combined efforts of tenured astronomers and rookie, college-grad-scientists that are aspiring to be the next Neil Armstrong, Carl Sagan, or Stephen Hawking, mankind takes giant leaps toward understanding the universe a little more.

By the way, do me a favor and never put a boundary on the aspirations of your future. I mean, as long as it doesn't involve like, becoming a mass murderer or something. In that instance, I'm reminded of the words of one of my best friends, Mr. Wayne Workman. You see, I once asked Wayne the question about what the correct education is. His response, although short and simple, provided more truth than any text book definition out there. Wayne said, "It's not the education that hurts or helps. It's what you do with that education".

What he was basically saying was that reading up on how to make a bomb out of ammonia nitrate and diesel fuel is perfectly fine. It's a bad idea to attempt to perform that action unless you're in the demolition business. Wayne was also the one that helped trigger the idea of making moderation and balance a part of everyone's life. The idea of balance, in regards to education, is that it's great to study and learn about something that you're interested in, but you shouldn't limit yourself to only that area of study. When you do that, you unknowingly make yourself closed-minded because you're only willing to see one thought.

Physics is an area of science that is very common among astronomers. So if you're studying up on astronomy, you're bound to inherently learn some physics as well. It's also the gateway to astrophysics, the step-brother of astronomy. Physics combines advanced mathematical formulas to other areas of science such as chemistry, astronomy, geology, and every kind of engineering you can imagine.

Come to think of it, there aren't really any areas of science that don't require mathematics. A little food for thought, statistically speaking, the more math you learn, the more money you will earn. If you're making all of that money and you don't want to be as stupid as I was in my youth, you might want to consider reading up on economics. I think at one point in my life, my credit was so bad that when I sent off a request to find out my score, all I received was the phone number to the suicide hotline and a message saying "Hey, keep your head up; things will get better, I promise". So if you don't want to end up in that situation, you owe it to yourself to study up on some economics. Besides, who wouldn't want an extensive understanding of how to build a successful stock portfolio? That way, you don't have to pay someone else to do it for you and you can save even more money.

Biology is another great science to study because it touches on so many more concentrated areas such as oceanography, botany, zoology, pathology, medicine . . . . Well actually, pretty much every area of the medical field, considering biology is a life science. Nurses, surgeons, and internists usually all have extensive background in anatomy, physiology, mathematics, chemistry, and biology. And if you're thinking, "That all sounds really difficult" or "Why would I want to learn that? I'm never going to use that", allow me to rectify that misconception. Why would learning about sickness or injury, and how to treat it, ever be a bad thing? And not just for yourself, but also for your children and your family. And again, not to sound shallow, but most medical fields usually pay pretty well.

If you're reading this book in your spare time, between sleeping and flipping burgers at the local fast-food restaurant, I sincerely hope you will treat this section with extra attention and perhaps take action in the appropriate direction. I don't think video games or television are bad, in moderation. I know I enjoy them. But please do society a favor and take a few minutes, from your hectic schedule of button mashing, to read up on the complexity of the human eye and its connection to the brain. While you're at it, take a quick look at the unfathomable perplexity of the entire central nervous system. If you're not completely blown away with what you discover, I'm guessing you're either illiterate or high off your ass.

Society openly jokes about students that major is philosophy in college, or proceed even further to the master's and doctoral levels. For anyone that didn't go to college, the "Ph" in PhD has nothing to do with the proper balance of acidity levels. It stands for doctorate of philosophy. Anyone with enough successful college classes can receive a doctorate level degree. However, PhD's are all advanced, thesis-based degrees. The origin of the word philosophy comes from it's Greek ancestors, who created it, meaning "love of wisdom". That's a stereotype that most philosophical thinkers won't argue with because most of them take pride in it.

To receive a PhD your compiled thesis work has to be accepted for publication. PhD's usually are put together with other PhD's and have their works inserted in text books, and informational magazines. Again, I'm not saying that a PhD is better; it's just different and usually a little more difficult to earn.

Ask a doctor of any social science for example which pads more on a resume, and I'm pretty sure you'll find the answer more unanimous than ambiguous. That's why almost any PhD out there would probably argue that philosophy is an important area of study. It favors strong analytical process coupled with deductive reasoning as opposed to inductive reasoning. It's problem solving, and that's a skill that you can use in almost any career field. Most professionals don't want to hear your reason for making a difficult decision was either, "It seemed like a good idea" or "It's what my dad would have done".

Along with the social science professionals, pretty much every law student will tell you the value and importance in studying philosophy. The Socratic Method, stemming from the man who created philosophy, is one of the primary and most common areas of study taught at any law school. Ever see a lawyer throw 35 questions at a defendant on trial? Many of the questions force the person on trial to contradict themselves. Ever wonder what the lawyer is doing? They are most likely practicing the fundamentals of Socratic Method. God knows there's never been a more twisted moment than the guy standing on trial that is asked, "Do you still beat your wife like you used to? No, you don't? So you beat her in a different manner now than you used to? Hmmm? Interesting?"

Even if you don't get your college degree in philosophy, you can still study it. Hell, you can read up on it from home and learn just as much as you could at school. All of the great free thinkers of the world are the living body of that which we call philosophy. Putting it more plainly: free thinking means being open-minded. That may be one of the reasons why philosophical thinkers have a tendency to not conform to any one religion, if they are spiritual at all. They approach everything in life with an open mind, and they are generally more logical and less prone to quickly pass judgment.

Time

Time can change everything we know
What we would praise today as knowledge
We would have deemed witchcraft before
We now realize was a mistake
What was thought as the end of the world
In time was found to be false
And rules of science that were thought impossible
In time were proven to break
And the true wonder of time
Is the knowledge that we gain from the past
To prove for a better tomorrow
So our children may enjoy their today
And the struggle that our fathers have felt
Was to be sure that we would live on
And carry on the names of the past
And open our minds to brand new ways

In the most recent years technology has moved ahead by leaps and bounds. Just imagine where humanity could be if everyone was educating themselves further, rather than sitting at home doing nothing.

You can be rich or poor and still be educated. While a college degree may help you land a job and make more money, it's never an excuse to think you can't learn more. You can be born into the wealthiest family in the world, but if you spend your whole life thinking you are better than anyone else and don't need to educate yourself, then I just feel sorry for you. Remember boys and girls:

Moral of this story: Education is the bridge between ignorance and understanding.

CHAPTER 15

Diplomacy . . . .

(Which Is . . . Getting Your Diploma, Right?)

Diplomacy—n. 1. the practice or art of conducting international negotiations. 2. tact and skill dealing with people.

How many people know what diplomacy really means and why it is important? I always seem to end up connecting diplomacy with the United Nations when I try to explain it to people.

Everyone that I talk to seems to think that the U.N. is nothing more than a country club for the men and women that ultimately decide what to do for the countries of the world. Supposedly, in the case of any international endeavor, disaster, or combined governmental effort, the appropriate members of U.N. meet and discuss how to go about the situation as safely and **diplomatically** as possible. My, what a charming fairy tale version of the truth.

The reason the U.N. is getting labeled as a country club is because at the present time there is no imminent international threat overhanging the U.S. or any other number of multiple countries. Right now, there is the war on terrorism; that's about it. To make things worse, terrorist attacks are random which makes calculating them very difficult to intercept, if not impossible. Then you have to factor in the issue of attacks involving multiple countries.

I doubt very seriously if 1% of the U.S. could tell you who six members of the U.N. are; they probably couldn't even tell you six members of Congress are. Do you know what that means? That tells me that if a serious international incident were to occur, nobody would know who was making the decisions for them. That's kind of sad. I know, I know. You can't expect people to know everything. I'm not suggesting that. I'm suggesting people know just a fraction of it.

Right now the population of America and potentially the rest of the world doesn't care because society still has its humanity (or at least as much as we had before). But the moment the shit hits the fan, you can bet people will start to care who is telling them who is going to live and how they are going to live.

But honestly, this section is not meant to discuss the purpose of the U.N. This chapter of the book is dedicated to explaining why I feel diplomacy is important in the world, especially in our own country. Diplomacy is an idea, not a convention. It's philosophy, not a "Comic Con". I think every citizen of humanity should educate themselves on diplomacy; from the lowest member, all the way up to the officials that govern our countries. If mass chaos does ever break out, it would be nice to know that humanity as we know it has the means to maintain its civility and continuity of our societies and governments.

Yes, I can already hear the insults flying through the air, calling me ridiculous or insane for even thinking that could ever happen. Or perhaps it's more correct to say that I want humanity to survive itself and diplomacy may be the only way. Everyone always values the need for diplomacy after it is already too late.

Humans are growing more technological every year, and yet one of our most basic instincts is to destroy ourselves. When people panic our destructive nature becomes amplified exponentially. Part of that being the fear of death and the desire for survival which can make people we would normally consider very level and rational, commit some very scary and irrational actions. People turn on each other in the face of desperation, and I would like to see a world that could survive the hysteria and madness of a post-chaotic world. Is it far-fetched? Yes, but I'm speaking idealistically.

Chance seems to favor the prepared. So why not be prepared? There are so many possible end of the world situations that society is concerned with. The depleting ozone layer, the polar ice caps melting, an asteroid the size of Oklahoma hurling toward Earth to wipe out all of humanity, a coronal mass ejection large enough in scale to do the same thing, artificial intelligence being created and becoming self-aware, an alien invasion, nuclear war, and of course, the good old-fashioned end of the world scenario brought to you by the Mayan calendar, are all centered around the theme of human annihilation.

So with this scary world outlook in your mind, remember what the Boy Scouts of America say: "Make sure to pull the chicken out of the freezer when I get home so that it can have time to thaw for tomorrow night's dinner with . . . ." Err . . . . my bad. Sorry, I was doing two things at once and kind of lost my train of thought there. But uh . . . I don't know where I was going with that. But yeah, do . . . . Whatever it was I was saying earlier. And now I have this sudden craving for chicken for some reason.

Moral of the story: Don't think about more than one thing at a time while I'm writing.

CHAPTER 16

The Holocaust Sucked

Now is the part of the book where I go into a little more depth about the Holocaust. Sure, I could spin a literary web of ire directed at Nazi Germany from 1939-1945. But why? That would make me no better than somebody persecuting me for something that my great grandfather did to their family. Plus, it's probably nothing that hasn't been said in 1,000 other books.

I could probably insert a halfway decent short story depicting the trials and tribulations of a Holocaust survivor and the unspeakable acts that he was subjected to during his time in a concentration camp. The problem with that is, it makes it seem as though I'm demonstrating bias on behalf of Jews, and not humanity itself.

I could reference endless statistics from the thousands upon thousands of pages that have been documented by well-known PhDs. But if you really wanted that, you could just read all of their books, couldn't you? Instead, I am going to discuss why we, as citizens of humanity, can never allow it to happen again. If I want to be fair, it's best to just stick to supporting my own opinions with facts. English Comp 101.

I've asked several closed-minded people to put themselves in the shoes of the person, or group of people, they are persecuting. I place emphasis on this idea because so much unnecessary hatred could be avoided if people practiced this more often. The next time you see someone wearing a Star of David and go straight to, "God should wipe all Jews off the face of the Earth for killing Christ", try taking a second to think about the fact that that Jew was <u>BORN</u> a Jew. He or she had no control over who their parents were. If that person converted to Judaism, it's probably because that religion makes the most sense to them. So, in that sense, they are no different than you. That person's religious preference has no effect on you living your life.

If you do happen to be from a religion such as Christianity that isn't exactly fond of the idea of the Jews killing the deified idol known as Jesus Christ of Nazareth, please try to remember:

1) Your God told His son it was going to happen
2) God is in control of everything. So, I'm pretty sure if He didn't want His son to be murdered, He wouldn't let it happen.
3) Jesus was, in fact, **A JEW!** I can just see how it must have been way back then. When Joseph needed carpentry supplies, he just sent his "Step-Son" Jesus to the market. Jesus being the typified Jew probably purchased the cheapest materials and tools he could find.

But hey, if you can look at all of those ideas and still want every Jew to die, you are too far gone for anything I am going to say to really make a difference. If that's the case, then by all means, give this book away to someone who still has a functioning brain. I know my random and sporadic thoughts can make it difficult for me to stay on topic, but if you are willing to stick with me just a little longer, I'm getting there; I promise.

Let's wind the clocks back about a century and investigate where the intolerable hatred from the former Commander of the Third Reich, originates from. A certain Nazi leader by the name of Adolph Hitler, who was known as "Adi" in his youth, rose to power, ended up commanding the Third Reich, and mercilessly killed 11 million or so men and women including somewhere between 6-6.5 million Jews. He did so by becoming the chancellor of Germany in 1933 and gaining command of the German military (even though he was actually born in Austria). This form of persecution is known as genocide, and it was devastating. It was led by one single man who had an idea to take over the world by force and annihilate anyone that wasn't a white Christian.

I wonder how many people truly died in the Religious Crusades. I mention that again because the Crusades share many of the same traits as the Holocaust. Yes, Hitler did some unspeakable acts to even his own people if they turned against him, but is it really any different than when the Catholic Church went on a mission to spread what they felt was the law and the truth and killed anyone who disagreed with them? No, it isn't.

Here's a few pieces of the Hitler puzzle that many people do not know. Hitler wanted all Jews killed, plain and simple. But let's slow down for a second and try to analyze why. There is no 100% confirmed reason why Hitler hated Jews the way that he did. Try reading *Mein Kampf* for a start though. It explains how Hitler developed his theory of the Jews seeking ultimate control over the entire world. Yeah, that makes sense. They're not allowed to do it, but Hitler can. Sure. There are several theories for this. One theory (that is unfortunately speculation at the moment) is that Hitler had Syphilis. For those among you who did not have health class, Syphilis is a nasty little sexually transmitted disease that he contracted while with a Jewish girlfriend (and by girlfriend, I really mean a prostitute from Vienna), in 1908.

Syphilis is especially bad because not only does it kill you, it kills you by slowly eating away at your brain causing massive functional problems. So that's one reason he could have possibly held on to his hatred for the Jews. Some psychiatrists believe that if Hitler had the disease, it could also explain his desire to eliminate the mentally retarded.

Another semi-recent theory is that Hitler's grandfather was Jewish. Whoa, what a mind job, right? So then, why would a man raised by a Jewish father kill all of these innocent people? It could very well be that this Jewish father abandoned his little Anti-Christ son and left him with some severe daddy issues. But once again, that is only a theory. Another common idea comes from Hitler's mother, who unfortunately was diagnosed and ultimately died of breast cancer. The diagnosis came from the family Jewish doctor. This situation poses the idea that Hitler blamed the Jewish doctor for not doing his job correctly, which may have inadvertently led to his mother's death. So we could potentially have a Jewish hooker that gave him a life-ending STD, a father who is Jewish and abandoned him as a child, and a Jewish doctor who diagnosed and delivered the news that left Hitler's life literally shattered henceforth. But the most well-known and documented is his belief in the conspiracy theory that the Jews secretly were plotting to take over the world completely, beginning with the financial institution and then slowly, destroying Hitler's ways of life that he had come to know.

And that is just a few of many more factors feeding into an intolerable hatred throughout his life. He's a complicated guy that we don't really have much history on. This might be a good time for one of my favorite poems that I've ever written.

The Innocent

For years the Innocent lived in harmony
Then all at once their families were torn
Their life of freedom was taken away
And in that moment a prisoner was born
Aware of their fate they prayed for a swift death
Branded with more than burden and disdain
The branding them too was an unwarranted crime
That was brought to the Innocent in the Fuhrer's name
They trudged through the mud in their tattered clothes
Seeing those before them that have died
They waited in fear of their number being called
With no hope for escape and nowhere to hide
The intolerable hatred that punished the innocent
With acts of cruelty as often as the rain
That forced fathers and sons to separate
And released death upon the world in the Fuhrer's name
There was no light at the end of the Innocent's tunnel
Nor was there even a tunnel for them to find
Instead there was pain in the absence of hope
And visions of the repeated war crimes
The screams of the Innocent carry on through the night
Like a broken record that played the sound of pain
But the screams fell on deaf ears every time
While orders were carried out in the Fuhrer's name
The images were burned in the minds of the doomed
And the Innocents cried out in a state of terror
Skeletal bodies withered from starvation
Enduring a fate that no one should bare
Neither women nor children could find sanctuary
Because genocide is unbiased and gilded with blame
And all were found guilty in the court of the Third Reich
And quickly put to death in the Fuhrer's name

Again, we don't know everything about Hitler's childhood. Maybe he actually hated his father because his dad made him eat Lima beans and tell him he liked them, or maybe he just neglected Hitler so much that he was warped from the get go. I don't know, I wasn't there. But if any or all of those examples did happen, it sure would make for a recipe for disaster.

Let me just say before I get into my next rant that in no way do any of the things that I just listed condone killing even one person, let alone 11 million. What a Nazi bastard! If there is a Hell, I hope he's down there watching *The Home Shopping Network* 24 hours a day, while having his skin removed with 50 grade sandpaper over and over again. OK, I've said my piece. Now we can move on.

Moral of the story: Don't kill the Jews. Seriously, that's just stupid.

CHAPTER 17

Religion . . . . Where Do I Begin?

This is a warning that this section discusses one of the most controversial mainstream ideas in the world. Approximately half of this book deals with religion in one way or another, so you should know that before you read on. What I'm about to begin and go into for quite a while is not for the judgmental or the fanatic of either side. I'm going to dive into a bunch of points that I have problems with, and points that other people have brought to my attention that I happen to agree or disagree with. And I'm not just talking about the Catholic faith either. I'm going to get into quite a few religions, and I will probably bounce around like a kid with ADHD that hasn't taken his medicine for a few days because, that's just who I really am. With that being said, let's begin.

I discussed indoctrination previously in the beginning of the book. Because indoctrination plays such an integral role in religion, I will be making note of it off and on, throughout this entire section of the book that deals with religion. If a person is uneducated about a religion, gang, church, or any other organization, they should learn all about it before they become committed to something that could be leading them down a very dangerous path. Furthermore, forcing religion on your children is morally wrong.

How can we be so naïve as to think that ordering our children to believe something that we want is ever going to be real? Even if children are forced into joining a particular religion or church, it wouldn't be them making their own educated decision. For that reason, it will never be real. As an infant, it's not as important because the children are not aware of what is going on enough to have an opinion to voice. But as children reach adolescence, they need to be able to begin making educated choices for themselves.

As parents we want what is best for our children. But please let your kids make up their own minds about what makes sense to them. Otherwise, they will just end up sitting in the church, watching the clock, and trying to not fall asleep. What's worse, they may grow up hating church or even the idea of God. I know many of you are thinking, "I want my kids going to my church and growing up with proper morals". That is great. I believe church is a place to learn a lot of really good morals. I also think it's a great place to go to make yourself feel better so you can go do more bad things again.

I grew up as a Christian, or at least I thought I did. I suppose in reality, I grew up as one of the people I describe quite often in this book. I called myself a Christian even though I didn't know anything about the Bible. I didn't know about Jesus Christ, and I was constantly counting down the minutes to the end of the church service, on the occasions that I did attend.

I happen to think I am a very morally sound individual. In fact, more so than most people that I know, many of which call themselves Christians. No, I do not have a degree in English, philosophy, theology, or political science. However if they were handing out college degrees for understanding and reasoning or logical thinking, I would probably have a degree in any or all of those.

Moral of this story: Whoever created religion must have had a father and mother who were also brother and sister.

CHAPTER 18

How Old Are We?

One of the most common discussions I have with people is debating the most accurate age of the Earth. There are arguments on both sides of the spectrum when discussing the Earth's age. On one hand, we have Anno Mundi (AM), which quite literally means "in the year of the world". Religious scholars on both sides seem to agree that the Earth is no more than approximately 5,500 years old, as it is defined in the Septuagint. The Hebrew Masoretic text suggests that the Earth could be as young as 4,000 years old.

By the way, just food for thought, the Vulgate was translated and written in the 4th century A.D., and it is the Latin translation of the Septuagint, the Greek translation of the Hebrew Bible, created at the end of the 3rd century B.C. It was the cornerstone that was used to create the Gutenberg Bible, the first printed press Bible that went into wide circulation. Did you really need to know that? Probably not. But I just love putting little facts like that into my writing. It helps break away from the monotonous banter that I can start to drone on about after a while. I also do it to educate anyone that will actually humble themselves enough to read my crappy writing.

Getting back on topic, these religious experts estimate the age of the Biblical Earth by calculating the ages of the individuals in the Old Testament; then when they reach the New Testament, more specifically the birth of Jesus Christ, they simply add the number of years A.D. we have had to the first number. These calculations were made under the Julian and Gregorian calendars.

It's probably a good idea to note that in the Old Testament, (Genesis especially) mankind lived a lot longer than we do today for some reason. For example, according to the Book of Genesis in the Holy Bible, Noah, Seth, and Methuselah each lived to be over 900 hundred years old. I find that fact interesting considering the average life span back then was lower than it is today. Historically, variables such as illness and infection killed off millions of men and women at an early age because of a lack of medical knowledge. So, it just doesn't add up when you say that these men lived hundreds of years longer than they do today. That makes about as much sense as saying that humans were 10 foot giants 5,000 years ago, when archeology shows us that humans were dominantly shorter in height than they are now. And since people apparently like to make shit up on a whim, let's ask Captain Logical to tell us some more historical "facts".

"Captain Logical, what other facts should we know?"

Captain Logical: "Humans used to be able to fly by flapping our arms really fast. The average male penis was 2 and a half feet in length. The earliest humans were blue in color and dreamed of one day having a movie called *Avatar* modeled off of them. No, we don't have any evidence to back that up, but don't worry, it's OK. We don't rely on foolish ideas like . . . proof."

Yes, sarcasm is my second language. However, if you do believe every word of the Bible, then you can always play the trump card of "All things are possible with the power of God". I know there are those that find what I think ridiculous. That's fine. That is everyone's right. I am also fine with believing that people that think I am ridiculous are delusional. I can think whatever I want; it doesn't mean that I feel any of these delusional people are bad. I just think they're delusional.

I am not sure of the person who made this quote, but I hope he is not on a jury anywhere deciding the fate of someone's life.

"There are many lines of evidence that the radiometric dates are not the objective evidence for an old Earth that many claim, and that the world is really only thousands of years old. We don't have all the answers, but we do have the sure testimony of the Word of God to the true history of the world." (Unknown)

Really? That makes no sense. Basically you are telling me that you are basing all of your facts from a fictional book, or a collection of books really, of which no one can validate the actions that took place in the stories. What's worse is that you are saying you have the sure testimony of a divine body with which you have no direct line of communication. I know that you don't because I don't. I'm pretty sure I'm just as human as anybody else.

It is amazing to me that God would let one man be able to talk to him and not every man and woman. You can't make outrageous statements like this quote and expect anyone of a true intelligence to respect you because you're contradicting yourself constantly. As long as there are hypocritical, closed-minded people in the world that will make statements like this, the world will always be light years away from understanding so much as 1% of anything outside of our world. I am not saying that you shouldn't believe in God or any religion for that matter. What I am saying is that if you are going to believe in something, you should have answers to logical questions. You should research, learn, and understand what it is you are trying to defend.

Here's a thought. If God created all things, he must have created dinosaurs right? We know dinosaurs exist no matter what people try to say because we have the scientific evidence to fully support it. I guess I just can't see Noah getting all of the creatures of the Earth on the ark. I wonder how it looked getting to see Noah luring all of the animals in. The platypus, the snake, the spider, the giraffe, the Tyrannosaurus . . . . Wait, what? Oh yeah, since we know dinosaurs existed, but we're also supposed to believe everything that the Bible tells us, I suppose there was also every kind of dinosaur on board the ark as well. And we all know how well Tyrannosaurs play with others. Or no . . . That's right . . . . They don't.

Maybe we've been getting it wrong all this time? Perhaps the authors didn't translate the Vulgate and the Septuagint correctly. All this time we've believed that Jesus went into Nazareth riding on an ass. When the truth is he clearly must have gone riding into Nazareth on a <u>VELOCIRAPTOR</u>. That makes much more sense. There, crisis averted. Now we can go on believing the Bible and don't have to deny the existence of dinosaurs. If that's not a diplomatic solution, I don't know what is.

We have fossils found in pretty much every country, presenting the idea that they ultimately covered the whole Earth. Then there's a little thing called radio carbon dating. This should be a very household word by now. But just in case, radio carbon dating is taking a machine that generates radioisotope carbon 14 to determine ages as far back as 60,000 or more years ago. Going far beyond what any religious text claims the Earth to be.

Of course when religious fanatics are approached with this, they completely deny it, claiming that the use of this kind of technology is faulty or inaccurate. The funny thing is, when they used radio carbon dating to find the accurate age of the Shroud of Turin, the alleged linen that covered Jesus of Nazareth and burned his image into it, it gave a 95% positive analysis that the shroud was dated to 1260-1390 A.D. So, I wonder why religious people would say that carbon dating is faulty.

So what does science have to say about the age of the Earth? If you go by radiometric meteorite dating in comparison to lunar samples used to calculate everything down to the creation of our solar system. Yeah, I know what you are thinking right about now (at least the scientists out there). You're probably saying that the Earth was formed around 4.6 billion years ago (4.567 billion years, to be exact).

So 4.6 billion years ago, the Earth was created right? Why not? So what happened then? If you believe the science part, the Earth was a lifeless planet, filled will hydrogen gas and helium, random earthquakes and lots of volcanic activity. Ultimately, not very appealing to the eye. But let's go ahead and jump a billion years into the future. Guess what? There's plant life now, and waters that cover pretty much the entire Earth. From there, plant life evolved into creatures, very primitive and probably none of which containing a backbone. But at this point the Earth is at least a little easier on the eyes. Fast forward even further.

Now we've reached the Triassic, Jurassic, and Cretaceous periods, approximately 250-350 million years ago, which brought the dinosaurs that I spoke of earlier. The dreaded T-Rex, "the Lizard King", that was able to rip apart other dinosaurs with his teeth, little hands that were more for decoration, and a head that looks like it was designed from a caricature. Big dinosaurs, little dinosaurs . . . . Tall, skinny, medium, vegetarians, and burger-eaters alike. Much more intelligent than the previous organisms moving about the Earth but still unable to last forever. What happened exactly?

Well I'm sure at this point, everyone knows the asteroid theory. A big rock, approximately six miles in diameter (just in case you were wondering) collided with the Earth. There's a little speculation in regards to the size of the asteroid, but it's irrelevant. I wasn't there. And for that matter I'm glad I wasn't. Because according to scientists, it wiped out everything including dinosaurs, plant life, and even bacteria.

It's depressing I know, but luckily none of us had to be around for it. By the way, for anyone out there that actually gives two shits, we know exactly where the asteroid that wiped out the dinosaurs hit. So, for anyone that says that it never happened, you can shut up. Look it up for yourself. It's called the Chicxulub crater.

Where was I? Oh yeah, pretty much everything alive was incinerated with the heat blast that covered the Earth. For the math wizards out there, we do not possess enough modern-day nuclear weapons on the entire planet to cause that kind of destruction. The second disaster, following the heat blast, was mile high tsunamis all around the globe. Places like Australia, the coasts of the Americas, Japan, China, etc. would have been wiped out as the oceans of the world literally blanketed whole countries.

But it gets worse, because, at that point, the Earth was covered in a cloud of ash and dust that couldn't be penetrated by our sun. So naturally, what do you think happened? Everything froze. Thus, the wonderful dawn of the Ice Age, or at least one of them. The Ice Age is an idea that has spawned Hollywood movies, probably a dozen history specials, and again since no one was there, gave the asteroid and dinosaur theory some closure. Nuclear winter is a real bitch by the way, because any life forms or dinosaurs that would have survived starved to death because everything else was killed in the heat blast or the tsunamis, leaving no other dinosaurs to eat or plant life alive.

Which brings this ridiculously long story to the next higher mammal, primates. Walking around with no opposable thumbs, all the while swinging from trees, eating bananas, flinging poo, and having as much ape sex as their monstrous sized hearts could allow. Wait a minute, I think I can already hear religious fanatics picketing outside my window. Nope, never mind, that's just hail. That's right! Scientists believe without question, we came from a monkey. That seems hard to come to grips with for a very large majority of people. But for this section of the book, we're going to believe it, OK?

OK, moving ahead a bunch, (40,000 B.C.) introducing Cro-Magnon A.K.A. "The Cave Man". Looked a lot like a hunchback, speaking in mostly grunts and yelling, and jumped up and down at the creation of primitive cave paintings and the invention of small, flint tools. And when you stop to think about it, deservedly so because that was probably the dawn of technology. So they walked around the Earth until about 15,000 BC.

Now we'll call it the age of reason, or maybe not, depending on which side of the fence you happen to be swinging for. The world as we know it was born. And with it came mass destruction in every way as man began to enhance his knowledge and increase the numbers which inhabit this now green and blue, beautiful world.

Back in the day, and I don't mean Vietnam, humans were simple creatures. We probably believed anything that anyone said. That's a dangerous way to build your ways of life, following anyone that claimed they were knowledgeable about something. But mankind did it. In fact, mankind still does it to this day. I'll even demonstrate what I mean. A study was conducted in New Hampshire and found that one, out of every four Americans is currently living with an STD. Can you believe that? I sure hope not. I don't even know if that's true. I just made that shit up. But people naturally want to believe other people that even remotely appear to know what they are talking about, rather than conduct their own research to validate the information.

Back to the topic at hand, right around 4,000 BC the different lands around the world began becoming dominated by civilizations. With each civilization came the religions that explained their existence, their origin, their ideas about an afterlife and moral guidelines and rules. Each one endowed with infinite faith and each one believed without question by its people. Why do you suppose civilizations naturally create the stories of creation, afterlife, etc.? Realistically, humans have a natural sense of wanting to answer questions such as where did everything come from? What happens after you die? What is the meaning of life? Why do bad things happen to good people? How do I pick the winning lottery numbers? For some of us, that last one could answer the meaning of life question.

There are literally hundreds of connections between religions from all around the globe, some dating back to ancient Sumeria and China. Civilizations throughout time all have similar stories. Norse, Greek, Roman, Egyptian, Judeo-Christian, Aztec, Mayan, Hindu, Dao, and Native American religions all have their own stories. Many of these religions have their own religious text such as the Bible, the Qur'an, the Tanakh, and the Mahabharata (the Hindu religious text).

Dozens of religions have stories of a great flood that wipes out all of humanity as a punishment for the wickedness of man. Even more have correlations on their views of some sort of Hell where people are sent after they die for their wrongdoings on Earth. The great flood that is mentioned in all of these texts may very well have happened in history. However, to think that it was because of God sending down 40 days of rain in a vengeful act of his wrath is just lazy.

The Chinese, Hindu, Native American, Judeo-Christian, the Mayans and the Aztec all have their own versions of how this story took place. Even the Sumerians tell a story of a great flood and the demigod named Gilgamesh that must escape it.

Scientists pose a theory that collectively answers how all of these cultures, spread all over the Earth, can have this one particular myth. Mainstream physicists, geologists, and paleontologists argue against a supernatural act of God. But you don't need to be a paleontologist to argue against that idea. All you need is logic. If there was a disastrous, end-of-the-world scenario, in which earthquakes began appearing in all of the oceans around the world, it would cause the majority of the Earth to flood and wipe out humanity. 1 + 1 = 2. This would explain how so many cultures on different continents share this same story, because the entire Earth was flooded. Then, the individual civilizations simply change the cause of the flood to fit their own religions.

It's not ridiculous to think that some of the stories in religions actually happened. But it's also not ridiculous to think that most of the stories can be explained through science. When cultures and civilizations don't understand something, their answer for it always seems to be "God". That's probably mostly because God doesn't require any reasoning or hard evidence. God simply is. That's all there is to it.

Moral of this story: It doesn't matter how old the Earth is as long as you're not around when the Earth is destroyed.

CHAPTER 19

Which Religion Am I?

How many religions are we talking about? Well to begin, let's dissect the different kinds. First, and primarily because of the time period, polytheism came much earlier than any of today's religions. Polytheism is the belief that multiple Gods control, dictate, and serve the world and all of its actions. Now, I could probably go on a rant, but for sake of your attention spans let's do the popular ones: Egyptian, Roman, and Greek. For the modern monotheistic religious believers, we have the Islamic, Jewish and Christian religions. Hopefully, I don't need to explain those, but I'm going to end up explaining it anyway. By the way, on a side note, I am doing my best to make this book idiot proof which shouldn't be too incredibly difficult considering I am writing it.

The Egyptians—Ra, God of everything under the sun. I say that because he was the sun god and eventually he jointly became the most powerful Egyptian god in their belief structure.

Some of the other popular Egyptian gods and goddesses are Horus, the ruler of the living world. His title carried with it many responsibilities such as maintaining a steady balance of the lands and its people. What makes religions such as Egyptian, Greek, and Roman mythology so interesting to me is that their Gods do more than bring life into this world or take it away. Their gods are unique in that they are usually all connected in one way or another with each other. For instance Hathor, the goddess of love in Egypt was also the wife of Horus.

Nut (actually pronounced Noot) was the goddess of the skies. She is responsible for the bringing of the new day, the giving of the rain for crops, and most importantly, she is responsible for being the watchful eye in the skies as a protector. Another important fact to remember is that many of the gods and goddesses in several religions and mythologies serve multiple purposes and can share the job of another god.

Anubis, another well-known god of Egypt, was the god of the dead and the god responsible for mummification. Gods in Egypt also can be violent according to their history. Brothers battled each other for control of more power, which actually explains why so many of the later gods of Egypt were a combination of two or even three gods and goddesses.

Anubis was also an integral part of the resurrection of men, pharaohs, and even gods. That brings up an interesting custom of the Egyptians, mummification.

In this horrifying act they separate the important organs of the body and place them in different jars or containers in order to preserve the things you will need when you move on to the afterlife such as the heart, the brain, (which is ripped out through your nostrils by the way) and even the male reproductive organ. The penis is actually traditionally stored with the heart. Personally, I thought it would make more sense to place the penis with the brain, seeing as those two organs are responsible for all male thinking. Mummification wasn't only performed by the Egyptian either. It was very common in other civilizations such as the Inca and the Chinese.

I would like to add one more thing about the Egyptians. They use pictures of their gods based on their assigned duties. For example, Nut is depicted as a blue female type holding up the skies with her arms, which basically looks like a big blue arch. Horus is composed of the body of a man and the head of a falcon in order to observe the lands and its living people. Anubis is made of the body of a man and the head of a jackal because at the time, the jackal was the creature that represented the dead. And of course Ra, the "Sun God" wild guess, the body of a man, head of some sort of big bird with the sun resting atop his head. Again, in case you're like me and have the attention span of an eight year old, we should probably move on.

OK. Moving along here, we've come to Greek mythology. Once again, I'm only going to cover a few of the main deities for the sake of time. And please remember, it is a very conflicting debate, but hopefully no one will come to my doorstep just to spit on me for expressing my thoughts. Getting back to our topic now . . . .

Let's begin with Zeus. The god of thunder, father of Apollo, Artemis, Athena, Dionysus and Hercules, the demigod (not to mention probably a few other dozen demigods considering how much Zeus liked to diddle the human women on earth). But even more than that, he is the supreme ruler over the world and all other gods. He is described as an understanding, loving god with great intention on maintaining the balance of the world. However, he is also mentioned as a force not to be taken lightly or insulted because he's likely to shove a lightning bolt up your ass. That would be like telling Chuck Norris that he fights like a little school girl in a pink dress.

Next on our short but educational list of deities is Ares, the god of war. This particular god really threw me when I read about him. He is the one who decides what will happen in battle. If you were victorious in battle, it was because Ares said so. If you lost in battle, it was because Ares said so.

People today would laugh at the idea of praying to Ares for help in battle, but praying to today's God for a safe return home and victory in battle makes sense for some reason. Yeah. So basically, believing in multiple gods that are responsible for individual actions of the world is Looney tunes. But believing that one god is responsible for everything is so much more rational. Anyone that actually believes that should get an "F" in Common Sense 101. "F" stands for "Fucking Stupid".

Aphrodite, the goddess of love . . . you know what, if this one isn't self-explanatory enough, you really need to do some reading. One interesting fact that many people don't know is that her son Eros is equivalent to Cupid in Roman mythology.

Apollo is our next candidate for dissection and explanation. He is the son of Zeus, and the god of music, the sun, and prophecy, as well as about a half a dozen other things that aren't really relevant to what we are talking about. Zeus was most proud of his son Apollo being born with the gift of prophecy because it was not your usual responsibility but more of a gift to use to help others. Plus, who wouldn't get excited about knowing next week's lottery numbers, right?

Athena was the goddess of wisdom, skill, trade, and battle strategy . Whenever a soldier learned to fight, or a farmer learned to farm, it was thanks to the guidance and offerings of Athena. Another small history note is the name of the city Athens in Greece is obviously named after Athena. She also had a fairly large statue in the city that was created in her honor. A pretty good compliment considering not too many of the smaller gods and goddesses got their own statues and cities.

Zeus' first brother Poseidon was the god of the seas and sat on a throne beside Zeus. Poseidon was extremely powerful and renowned for wrecking ships at sea when he was angry. Sounds more like a three-year-old throwing a toy on the ground when they're having a temper-tantrum if you ask me. When the people of Greece wanted to have a safe voyage at sea, they prayed to Poseidon. Poseidon's trident is also very recognized by today's popular culture, similar to Zeus' lightning bolt.

That brings us to Hades, the god of the underworld. He is generally envisioned as a bad guy and for good reason. Hades was sent to rule basically the same way the modern day Lucifer rules Hell. This of course would give more understanding to why exactly Hades bares so much anger for his two brothers because it was Zeus and Poseidon who tricked him into ruling the underworld. Again, I could probably go on and on about the other gods and their purposes, but it is just not germane to the topic of this book. That about wraps up the Greek gods. So, in honor of my ardent love for mythology, please enjoy these poems about religions and their Gods.

The Higher

Truth be told there is only one
The father of Apollo is king of all
Who bore his raw might with bolts of light
And kept watch with his eyes over all of the skies
Truth be told there is only one
Revered as "Optimus Maximus" by all
The brother of Pluto and husband of Juno
Who carried their long empire through years of fire
Truth be told there is only one
The Jade Emperor's word is law
Creator of the universe, master of the Earth
All knowing of the Dao but humble still to bow
Truth be told there is only one
The Sun God reigns over all as Khepri
Who gave us each new day and above all others we prayed
Worshiped more than any other, revered father and brother
Truth be told there is only one
Bhagavan holds all truth that is needed
Brahma when creating, Vishnu when he is aiding
And Shiva wreaked pain destroying in his reign
Truth be told there is only one
Creator of the Heavens and the Earth
Who sent his only son to Earth to save our souls upon rebirth
And banished the unholy foe to the fiery depths below
Truth be told there is only one

<u>Upon Their Thrones</u>

There were twelve that sat together on their thrones
Controlling the world as they saw was right
Raw power and beauty, wisdom and light
Even a gaze that would turn you stone
The king and his jealous queen would reign on high
But shared their home with their sisters and brothers
And while the king may have shared his bed with many others
He would always return his eyes to his queen
To his left and right were the weights of the balance beam
Upholding the order and life on his mother
And down in the depths was his vengeful brother
Whose home sat at the very end of the stream
On the thrones there was one who would bring the grain
And there was one that would forge the steel
One whose beauty defied anything real
And one in the moonlight who hunted for the game
There was one among them wisest of all
And one who waged war more than anything
There was one whose light and music would sing
And one who would guide the souls that would fall
There was one who commanded the waters between
And one who brought the gift of wine
There was one who was king of all the divine
And one, of course, to be his queen

Next on our agenda is the Roman gods starting with Jupiter. Now as you are about to see, the Roman gods are the same as the Greek gods. They just changed their names when the Romans became the commanding army and rose to power in Europe.

Jupiter is the exact same as Zeus. He has all of the same responsibilities and he is the supreme ruler just like Zeus. The only thing that's really different is that they each have their own stories and myths.

Apollo is interesting because not only is his name the same; he is almost the same god. Apollo is the Roman God of Light and God of the Sun. So because the similarities are so obvious, you can just refer back a couple of pages, and I can move on, can't I?

Venus, the goddess of love . . . .this is just text book, day one stuff again, people. However, you will notice again that she is the same as Aphrodite.

Cupid, I think everyone is familiar with the modern depiction of him. Oh, before I forget . . . . Cupid is a little more unique as he is listed as the god of "erotic" love. It sounds to me like the Romans really wanted to adopt the whole "freak in the sheets" persona.

What's next? Let me see . . . . Ah! Mars is the god of war, the same as Ares. Minerva is the god of wisdom, skill, trade and war; and you guessed it, the same as Athena. And last but not least, Pluto is the god of the underworld. AKA: Hades, to the Greeks. So that about wraps up your Greek and Roman gods. I'm trying to prevent myself from going into a rant on all of them and the times they reigned so that I can stay on topic.

Moral of this story: Six of one, half-a-dozen of the other.

CHAPTER 20

The End Is Near!!!!!

(Oh wait, no it isn't)

Earlier in the book I mentioned people panicking over the different ideas in which the world is going to cease to exist. Well, it's time for me to elaborate on a couple of them. There are so many end-of—the-world beliefs. Most of them are well-known because of their religious correlation. But in today's world, we have people in a panic over end of the world scenarios, and some of them don't even have anything to do with religions.

The Asteroid Theory—Everybody knows this one. But just in case, this is the theory that what happened to the dinosaurs will happen to us. If it does, we're all dead. There's really no need to give yourself a receding hair line thinking about the possibility of it happening. Although I'm sure the makers of Xanax will greatly appreciate you chewing your nails down to the bone over something that no one can control. I've heard people up in arms about the asteroid known as Apophis scheduled to collide with Earth with a 3% probability of impact. Yeah, that was true until the probability was moved to a 0% chance of impact.

For the doomsday enthusiasts out there reading this, perk up. There are approximately 20,000 near Earth objects (NEOs) capable of crossing paths with Earth's orbit and big enough to warrant concern. It's not for another 5,000 years. But, there are 20,000 potential NEO threats.

Economic/Civil Unrest—This Hellish idea centers on the premise that when gas prices and unemployment go up, so does the anxiety levels of the members of society. Well, OK. That part is true. People think that when shit gets out of control, the members of society will lose their civility and turn on one another. Your neighbors can no longer be trusted. In a nightmare like this, all you can think of is . . . ."My God, I've been loaning him sugar for years. How could he do this to me?" The truth is that in this unlikely event, martial law would be declared and the situation would be more than likely under control in a few days. Now the ugly aftermath of martial law is almost too painful to describe, but it's probably what it would take to fix the problem. I guess we should at least be glad that America has a plan of action for such an occasion.

2012—Is both an end-of-the-world myth and yet another one of my favorite movies. Let me say the only part of that sentence that mattered again. It's one of my favorite **MOVIES.** It's not real, people. So please, stop saying that it is. There are a few myths out there right now circulating and the closer we come to December 2012 the more the myths are gaining attention. Once again, people don't know the facts, and they're just giving out bad information.

You know, a guy at a music store tried to recruit me recently. He wanted me to join his team that he claimed he was establishing for the end of the world in December 2012. My first thought was a flashback of the year 1999 when everyone thought Y2K was the end of the world. I thought about telling him if he wanted to throw all of his money away like that on preparing for the apocalypse, he could give it to me. I have two daughters and mortgage payment that is overdue. But no, I didn't say that. Instead, I told him he was suffering anxiety over something that wasn't even there. Of course, he didn't listen, but I told him anyway. Besides, if the world was going to end, doesn't that kind of negate the whole need for preparation? Who the fuck wants to live in a world inhabited by . . . . Just you. No more friends. No more family. Nothing. Not to mention if the destruction wipes out humanity, you're problems are over, so why worry about something you can't change. Why not try and enjoy the time you have with your loved ones. I know it's not going to happen, and it's still putting me in a depressed state.

As far as the whole Mayan civilization myths, I'm only going to be going over the misconception of the end of the world running congruent with the end of their calendar because . . . . it's not the end of their calendar. December 21st, 2012 is the just end of the 13th baktun cycle of their calendar. There are 20 baktun cycles in the Mayan Long Count Calendar. A baktun is composed of 20 katun cycles which equates to approximately 144,000 days. That's all. The only reason anyone should think that the world is going to end on December 21st, 2012 is because according to Mayan legends, the last time the world was destroyed, it was at the culmination of the 13th baktun cycle. And even that is only mentioned briefly.

All I'm saying is, if you have a dentist appointment scheduled for December 22nd, 2012, I wouldn't cancel it if I were you. If you do cancel it because you think the world is going to end, all you are going to end up with is an ulcer caused from thinking about the end of the world too much and probably some cavities that could have been avoided. Actually, now that I think about it, it's currently June 6th, 2012. For all I know it may be two or three years before this book is even published. At that point, you guys can laugh along with me at all of the idiots who thought the world was coming to an end two or three years ago.

I've also heard other people talking about the world ending in 2012 because of a planetary alignment. If you're one of those people, I should make you send me a new pair of boots so that I don't have to ruin my shoes stepping in all of the bullshit that's coming out of your mouth. If you do some research, you will quickly discover that there is no such planetary alignment happening now or any time in the near future.

Solar Storms—This myth is actually more fact than fiction. Yes, it's true. Solar storms are a serious threat to our planet and the inhabitants walking around on it. It's also a fact that the sun goes through a heightened period of solar activity known as solar maximum every 11 years. Yes, it's also true that the radiation that is caused from solar flares and coronal mass ejections (CMEs) depletes the Earth's atmosphere. It has created the holes in the ozone and could be one of the causes of global warming. That's science. I still don't think it's anything to become completely hysterical over.

I didn't believe in global warming until recently. The documented evidence is difficult to ignore though. I'm from Missouri where there is a popular phrase among the residents of the state, "If you don't like the weather in Missouri, just wait five minutes." Lately, I think it should be changed to something a little more realistic. Something like, "If you don't like the weather in Missouri . . . . You should probably go ahead and move to Hawaii."

Regardless of the evidence, the activity on the sun is not going to be swayed in any way by your worrying. I do however believe that it would be a good idea for the government to begin preparing for solar storms knocking out the power lines and satellites all around the Earth. That's realistic. And frankly, I'm a little scared of a society without cell phones. American people without their precious cell phones to keep them connected to the world? I somehow picture that being more like a zombie apocalypse rather than a technological one. Which begs us all to question—What did everybody do before we had the ability to update FaceBook from our phones? How in God's name did we survive without being able to Tweet about the huge shit that we just took and how relieved we now feel?"

Moral of the story: People are going to believe whatever they want to believe. Moreover, people that love drama, aren't usually too picky when it comes to the kind of drama. I guess end of the world drama is just as good as "I heard her boobs are totally fake" drama.

CHAPTER 21

Merry Christmas Jesus

So the year is let's say, 33 AD. That's a good number right? Why is that a good number though? That's right, it was the year the lord Jesus Christ was crucified and rose from the grave. First thing, before we get started in a very long explanation of the modern day Christian faith, Jesus was not a Christian! I only say this because I have had more than one ignorant, uneducated moron who thinks that he knows everything, actually chime into a conversation that an associate and I were having, and decided to correct us by telling us that, "You know, Jesus was a Christian and not a Jew, right?"

Rather you're an Atheist, a Catholic, or a Jew, Jesus was not a Christian. Jesus was a Jew. If you want to be anal about it, he was actually from Galilee, in northern Israel. I promise. In fact, the term Christian actually means—A follower of Christ; or one who attempts to be Christ-like. So, it goes without saying by the very definition that Jesus cannot be a Christian because he does not follow himself.

I sometimes laugh when I think about the inconsistencies with people when it comes to their religion. One example I have learned to laugh at is the hatred that is spread in Jesus' name because of ignorance. People love to profess their love for God and Jesus. They will spend all day telling you that they are a Christian. And yet, for some reason, they can't tell you one thing about his life or even the Bible. So how then am I supposed to believe them when they say they are a Christian? It sounds more like they want to be accepted by society, and the majority of society calls themselves Christians.

Even if the people who say that they're Christians actually believe that Jesus of Nazareth is the Son of God, if they don't know anything about him, they're hypocrites and liars. I know basic math, and that's basic math. Trust me, I had to go all the way back and study it in college, remember? If you call yourself a Christian and you don't know anything about the guy, you're a liar. You are also pretty much the same as everyone else in society, so don't feel too bad.

The fact still remains however, if the previous statements describe you, you are believing in something that you know absolutely nothing about. If that's the case, you are unknowingly a victim of social conformity and indoctrination. Both of these could have been avoided if people could just take the ignorance variable out of the social equation.

Where was I? Oh yeah, that's right. The origin of Jesus. He was a Jew, plain and simple. His father was a Jew, just like his father before him. His ancestry includes some of the most important Jews in multiple religions, such as King David and Abraham. I felt like kind of an ass for doing it, but I had to correct that moron that said Jesus was a Christian. So, I acted like my usual sarcastic self by saying, "I'm pretty sure that INRI does not stand for the *KING OF CHRISTIANS*. I'm pretty sure it stands for the *KING OF JEWS*". So for all of the Jew haters out there, you might want to think about why you don't like Jews and make sure you're not persecuting a religion for the wrong reasons.

Let's go somewhere with what we were just discussing. Well, I'm discussing it. You're either reading this or using it for toilet paper or something to start a fire. The Jews seem to be hated by a very large number of religious enthusiasts for the merciless murder and crucifixion of Jesus Christ. But before you get all up in arms, let's stop and dissect that a little bit. They killed a man whom they believed to be passing himself off as the Son of God. Whether or not Jesus is the Son of God is irrelevant right now.

It's a little naïve and ironic to me because I'm pretty sure we do that sort of thing all of the time today. Wrongfully accuse an individual of a crime and then send him off with the death penalty, especially in Texas where everything from being gay to being an Atheist is enough to be crucified in their eyes.

Don't get me wrong, yeah, if they did murder God's only begotten son, that's a pretty bad guilt trip. But since we have no evidence of said argument, who is to say they are not being persecuted for the wrong reason? Maybe those who are holding a grudge against the Jews are wrong. Yeah, then what?

Another factor that is commonly unknown is that Jesus, a Jew, was going around and performing miracles on the day of the Sabbath. Performing miracles was expressly forbidden as it violated the 10 Commandments. Then again, I'm pretty sure nobody else was performing miracles at the time, so one would think that should have triggered some sort of alarm in their brains if the deification of Jesus Christ is true.

Moral of this story: Know what you're talking about before you open your big, fat mouth.

CHAPTER 22

The Definition of Hypocrisy

Hypocrisy—**1.** the practice of expressing feelings, beliefs, or virtues one does not hold or possess: INSINCERITY.

Generally speaking, a hypocrite is someone that tells you to act one way and then turns around and does the exact opposite. If you are going to believe in god, please actually believe in him/her/it. Live by sensible facts, love your God truly, spread the good word and believe without question. That's basically what most religions all have in common. They all require faith.

If you are a God-loving or believing individual, which religion then is the true one? That question can only be answered by you. The choice is yours. That's why it is called free will. You can choose to deny the very existence of God or choose to praise him with every ounce of your soul. But for God's sake, pardon the pun, do not force your religion on someone if they do not want to accept it. Forcing religion on someone is like making your kids eat those damn Lima beans that I mentioned before and then forcing them to tell you they like it. That worked out real good for Hitler didn't it? All you are doing is building up a slow, painful mental anguish that is going to grow to the point that when they can choose for themselves, they cannot stomach the word religion or any church practices.

No one can take your faith away or give it to you. It is something you decide. But to persecute another religion or non-religion such as a Muslim or an Atheist, makes you a hypocrite. If you question my opinion, perhaps you should take a quick peek at the Book of Matthew from the Bible.

Matthew 7:

1   "Judge not, that ye be judged."
2   "For with what judgment ye judge, ye shall be judged."

Rather you choose to accept the truth or not, if you are persecuting against another person's faith, practices, ethnicity, or life choices, you are the very definition of hypocrisy. Do you want to know why? Well rather you want to know or not, I'm going to tell you.

Allow me to use a historical example that everyone should be familiar with, the Religious Crusades, an enduring test of the strength of man in all his best efforts to save humanity. And how did they do that exactly? They went country to country and city to city and killed everyone that would not conform to the Catholic Church (all the while secretly masquerading as a front to conquer land and power). Because that's what God wants right? Obviously. Go and kill everyone that will not conform to the Catholic faith. I don't think that's what your God had in mind.

Regardless of what you read in any book, murder is murder. And if you can take two seconds to think about it, it is the exact same as forcing your child to eat Lima beans and tell you they like them. The only difference is there is a very slim chance that you'll end up dead if you don't eat Lima beans. But the analogy fits the same for both scenarios. I mean, do you really think that if you told me, or better yet, if someone told you that you are going to believe in Martians or else they will kill you, that you are going to honestly, all of a sudden, change your lifelong beliefs? Hell no! Chances are you're going to tell them whatever they want to hear as a means of survival at that point. But the belief structure is not something to toss around and expect true faith based on the infliction of fear. Whipping someone until they agree to believe whatever you say is not belief. It's just someone agreeing to do what you say out of fear of more pain being inflicted upon them. There's another common word for that. They call it slavery.

To make matters worse, falsely claiming your faith to God is hurtful and disrespectful to those that do genuinely love their God. I have a really hard time trying to picture an almighty, loving, caring and compassionate God that wouldn't be hurt when people lie and say they believe in Him. Speaking of **Him** . . .

Why is God referred to as a man in almost all scriptures? I'll tell you why. Because the Biblical books written by man in the word of God were <u>WRITTEN BY MAN</u>. At the time of the first documentation of God and His power, it was man's responsibility to maintain the day to day choices and even control when the women were allowed to speak. So naturally, God came out to be a man because men did all of the writing, and women had no place in the power of persuasion or decision making. And women think the men of today are misogynists. Try going back to those days for a quick minute. I mean, at least in today's world we have female authors like Anne Rice, famous for *The Vampire Chronicles*, J.K. Rowling, who wrote all of the *Harry Potter* books, and that chick who wrote all of those annoying, crappy, *Twilight* books.

I have news for anyone out there that actually believes that God is a man; He's not. End of story. I know what's going through some of your minds right now. God created man in His image, right? God has no image. That idea doesn't even make sense to me. But that's OK. I can have my own opinion. You don't have to agree with me. After all, you're entitled to your own stupidity.

That brings up another really good point. The Bible, the Qur'an, the Tanakh, etc. were all written by man. Written by man should set off big, bright, police lights that the Bible is fallible.

Now before your head explodes with anger and judgment, here me out. Say for instance, Bob from 3rd Street was around back in the day with God. Bob is a nut job that has a nasty habit of escaping from the local insane asylum. He believes he can talk to ghosts; he knows God personally and has seen Him with his own eyes and heard Him with his own ears.

It goes without saying that our friend Bob is off his rocker, like Mike Tyson near the end of his career when he was biting ears off. But Bob is one of the men that have a say in what is going to be put into the Bible or whatever religious book you happen to study. Now hundreds or even thousands of years later, because of organized religion based on fallible facts that got misconstrued, we have people worshiping something that was not true.

Another example came to me from my ex-wife Angel. I was writing a poem that was a shortened version of the Book of Revelations, chapters 6-8. She said if I were to bury my poem in some sort of sacred-like container and it were left for hundreds of years, who is to say a whole new faith isn't created from the discovery. I know the majority of society's conformists are probably getting heated right now, and I'm sorry. It just makes sense to me, and it's my God-given right (yet another pun) to believe whatever I want.

<u>The Beginning of the End</u>

The first was broken and I heard the voice
And a white-horsed-rider swept across the land
A sword appeared out of his mouth
And he carried a bow in the other hand
The second was broken and I heard the voice
Behold a red horse and a man with a sword
Who stole the peace away from the world
And turned man against man in war
The third was broken and I heard the voice
And riding in was a horse cloaked in black
And following with him was famine and disease
The punishment of man for our disobedient acts
The fourth was broken and I heard the voice
Behold the pale horse named Death
Who killed with the sword and the beasts of the earth
Who were released on those who were left
The fifth seal was broken and I heard the voice
But these were the voices of martyred men
Who cried out to God," Was our death in vain?"
And were bathed in good promise and white linen
When the sixth seal was broken so was the earth
And so a great earthquake shook the ground
And the sun and the moon were as shadow and blood
And the skies all began to fall down
Then twelve-thousand of the twelve tribes
Were marked with His name on their heads
And the rest were scarred with the mark of the beast
For sleeping in the dark lord's bed
And then every soul of man who accepted His gift
Wore the purest robes of white
And fell to the feet of the almighty king
To await their entry to the light
And when he broke the seventh seal

I thought only of His son's rebirth
And then in an instant all was calm
And there was silence across the earth

Moral of the story: "Do as I say, not as I do", should never be allowed to come from anyone's mouth.

CHAPTER 23

Stuck Between Iraq and a Hard Place

The Islamic faith is probably a good place to go to next. Holy Shit! You mean the psychos that crashed into the World Trade Center and the Pentagon? No, I mean the Islamic faith, which is closer to Christianity than most of the uneducated realize. By the way, it is the *Islamic* faith and *Muslims* are the adherents that follow the belief. And I'm sorry, but I do not blame the Muslim people for what happened on 9/11. I am a soldier in the U.S. Army so I know about pride in my country and when something like 9/11 happens I crumble inside, and I want justification right then and there. However, I am a realist, and I also know right from wrong.

If, by some happy twist of fate, there is a Muslim terrorist that gets to read this, please do me a favor and stop blaming all of your terrorist actions on your religion claiming that all infidels are being given their justice under your everlasting blanket of holy fire and blah blah blah. That is a big bag of bullshit and you and everybody else knows it. The worst part is that you are doing nothing but forcing thousands of good people on both sides to die in war over nothing.

The problem is one person is rational and understanding and can stop to think for themselves before they act. You get a whole country involved that was attacked by a different race, and you get what we have now, a bunch of angry, mob-like individuals that are willing to listen to someone of power and do just about anything that person says, much like religion as a whole. That's probably why religion and politics are the two most controversial debates we have ever known. Because in a way, they are closely related in how they are structured. They are both designed to control people. Except one of them gives people hope, and the other one . . . . forces you to pay taxes and go to war with whoever has the most oil.

So back to what I was saying, the Islamic faith deserves no spite or hatred from anyone. I refuse to put an entire faith or race on trial for the actions of few. Think of it this way; if your girlfriend gets raped in a back alleyway by a white guy, a black guy, a Muslim, a Jew, a Mexican, a Chinese guy and an Indian, are you going to hate every single race? That's impossible; so why would you hate any one whole race? That doesn't make any sense. Instead, what you should do is find every one of the guys that raped your girlfriend and beat the hell out of them for what they did. Actually, the really sensible thing to do is to turn them into the police, but personally, I'm just not going to feel very satisfied with that. While you're at it why don't you let someone steal everything in your home and force them to only give back 10% of what they stole before they can be released?

Islam is not as one-sided as you may think. There are actually two major groups of Muslims, the Shi'a and the Sunni. Each group has their own Hadith and each Hadith is not the same. Each Hadith claims to stipulate what Muhammad constitutes as approved or disapproved actions for Muslims. Because each Hadith has a different set of rules, the Shi'a and Sunni don't see eye to eye. Now I'll take all of that information and put it in simple terms.

Muhammad = Jesus (minus the Son of God part)
Shia = Catholics
Sunni = Protestants
Qur'an = the Bible
Hadith = different lists of what is right and wrong

Is everyone with me at this point? All Muslims have the Qur'an, which is very similar to the Holy Bible, and the Tanakh. Muslims believe that the Qur'an is the verbatim of God's word (Allah/God = same thing, just FYI). In fact, if you compared the Old Testament in the Holy Bible with the Islamic Qur'an, you could end up reading a lot of the same stories. The difference comes in the New Testament. They believe in following the guidance of a prophet named Muhammad, who lived from 570-632 A.D. and Muhammad was the last prophet of God. So instead of following one messenger/prophet of God, they're following another one. This simple explanation is a true testimony of sheep always looking to be led by a Shepard.

Muslims even believe that Jesus Christ existed. They just don't believe he is the Son of God. Sound familiar, like the Jews maybe? The irony is that the Islamic faith's most hated enemy is not American infidels. It is in fact . . . . Anybody that happens to be Jewish??? Wars, wars, and more wars. Thousands of years of wars. The reason behind that can possibly be explained in the Book of Genesis. I'll elaborate on that to offer more clarity.

Two brothers, Ishmael and Isaac, went their separate ways at a reasonably young age. One became a Jewish leader, and one became an Islamic leader. Each believed the other was wrong and was spreading the wrong message. More importantly, each believed that **his** people were God's chosen people. The hatred among the Jews and the Muslims has been carried on since the beginning of time, or the time in which the Book of Genesis took place, at least.

Yes, that is one of the main reasons people believe the constant feuding has never ended. There are of course other factors that have contributed through time, and the statement that Muslims hate all Jews or vice-verse is actually just a generalization. However, the point I was trying to make was that thousands of years of war have taken place because of these two men. It sounds bad, but it kind of makes me wish that Isaac and Ishmael had done the Cain and Abel thing. At least if they had done that, we may have only lost one life instead of millions.

How many people lost their lives because of the unforgiving hearts of two men? Two men whom by the way, may or may not have ever existed. That would be a goddamn shame, wouldn't it? The thousands of years of hatred and war may very well have happened over two fictional characters from a book. If you doubt the possibility, just show me their skeletons and I'll be more inclined to believe you.

It's ridiculous. Men and women growing up in a society that hates another religion, or being bred to kill another faith just because that's what your father and grandfather did, is as stupid as rival street gangs fighting amongst each other because of what side of the tracks they happened to grow up on.

It's been going on forever, and I don't see it changing any time soon. Which is a shame because we're missing out on all of the time that we could be using to figure out how to stop the zombie apocalypse. Yeah, didn't see that one coming did you? But instead, let's throw all of that away because it's what your friends are doing. Yeah, that makes more sense than basing your own decisions on facts and logic.

Now, I need to calm down for a second so I'm going to talk about something that many people live with every day. I'm talking about a giant web of lies that carries on like the O.J. trial with "Kato" Kaelin on the stand.

People of every faith commit the sin of lying to God. The way they do it is by acting as a hypocrite. There are way too many liars out there claiming to be living for God, or practicing good worship, or living by "the Book". When in reality, they could honestly tell themselves (because they won't admit it to anyone else) that they don't really care if God exists as long as they can live their life in peace. I really cannot stand social conformity.

I'll give you a couple of really good examples. Let's say you have a 35-year-old father taking his kids to church, and he tells his kids to pay attention to the sermon that is being given. The whole time before that, he was thinking about the delicious young female that is sitting next him in the pew; all the while, holding his wife's hand. Disgusting right? But it doesn't stop there, oh no . . . . later on that night he's drunk off his ass, and yelling at his wife and kids for absolutely nothing. Yeah, that guy is really living for God, right? Perhaps, **HE** should have been paying attention to the sermon.

A great number of people out there are going to church and feeling absolutely nothing during the service. They're just counting down the minutes until they can leave, and all along doing it so they can feel better about themselves.

If you're going to be for God, please be for God. If you're not for God, don't be for God. If that's the case, and you end up in Hell, at least you were real with yourself and everyone else while you were alive. Because if you're lying to yourself and everyone else, including God, I would venture to guess you're not righteously securing you're place in the Heaven that you don't really believe in. I have a lot more respect for someone that stands up and says, "I'm an Atheist!", or "I'm really a Muslim that is too afraid to stand up and say it because I'm afraid of being stoned to death by the people to my immediate left and right", than I ever would for someone that goes to church, lies to his family and the God he's supposed to be praising, and goes to bed at night with no problem.

I really do hope that there is a special place for people like that, where an angry and wrathful God can randomly look down at them, pull them out of Hell momentarily and say, "Well . . . . Maybe if you had actually believed in me . . . . I wouldn't have to do . . . This", and then send them right back to Hell.

For the Atheist out there that is feeling pretty self-righteous about him or herself, don't worry I'm going to roast you too later. As I briefly mentioned before, religion definitely serves it purposes. First of all, society as we know it would not and could not function like it has for so long without a spiritual following of some kind. It's a matter of moral guidelines.

Think about how many murderers, rapists, thieves, deadbeat dads, deadbeat moms . . . . Basically, criminals all around, that would not hesitate to do the things that they want to do or have thought about doing if there wasn't an eternal penalty for their crimes. The streets would be running wild with infinite madness and terror from sun up to sun down.

How many people are afraid of offing themselves because they're afraid they'll instantly burn in Hell for the rest of eternity for destroying God's temple? Well, the Catholics for one, but I know I don't want to either. Even if you're one of the hypocritical, closet-cased, non-believers, if there is a slight chance of eternal damnation for suicide, maybe you should just seek some help. Let's face facts, eternity is a long fucking time.

One of the many good things that are brought about by most religions is the hope of an eternity in Heaven. As an Atheist, I can speak first hand of the unpleasant feeling of emptiness that I've been filled with realizing that after I die, there is nothing else. That is a very depressing feeling. It also makes the idea of suicide much easier for someone like me because I don't have to worry about suffering after I die.

However, in retrospect it makes every single moment of my life much more meaningful because every moment could very well be my last. But if nothing else, please be logical. Don't do that to your family and your loved ones. Suicide, regardless of how bad you think your life is, is not the way to go. Death by orgasm, that's the way to go.

For the people like me out there that don't believe in God at all, all we have to do is follow governmental laws. For some, that's not a problem. For others that cannot maintain a good mental state long enough to get off parole, maybe you should move to Texas. That way you'll be so scared to even say the wrong thing to someone because you're afraid they'll strap you to a chair and make the lights go out.

If you're one of the murderers, rapists, thieves, or any other proud felons reading this, do us all a favor . . . . Stop. I mean every time I watch the news, I have to do all I can to not throw something at the picture of the guy that did whatever crime it happened to be. Rather it be parents leaving their babies in dumpsters or on the side of the road, or a man becoming enraged after walking in on his best-friend sleeping with his wife and kills them both, it's enough to almost force someone into alcoholism.

I'm getting to the point that I can't listen to the radio or watch TV. Seriously, any time one of my female friends wants to go out, they either have to go with like three or four other girls or take a guy friend and a buddy with them so that they will feel safe. You know what, that's pretty shitty. Because there are sick people out in the world everyone else is forced to walk on eggshells. It's the most repulsive act when the murderer, rapist, or child molester is one of the hypocrites that was in church that morning bragging about how on fire for God he is.

Oh, and don't worry. If he really does love God the way he says that he does, he's going to be on fire, all right . . . . When he's burning in Hell and trying to bargain his way back into the place he obviously wasn't interested in getting into. If these people were really interested in getting into Heaven they wouldn't have done what they did to deserve eternal damnation in the first place.

Sorry to fly off the handle like that again. I really was trying to calm down. So while I'm trying to drink this very delicious chilled coffee to relax, let's start a new topic. Terrorists are a good point. Oh my God! You mean the psychos that crashed into the World Trade Center and the Pentagon? Well, actually yes, this time. Supposedly, and I use that word lightly, the men responsible for the aircraft going down believed they were doing God's work, and that they would be a martyr and get 72 virgins. The same can be said for any of the martyrs that are suicide bombers, or any act where they yell, "Death to all infidels!", before they try to kill someone.

Does that mean that anyone who is a Muslim is going to try to attack people and kill them? No, it does not. And don't kid yourself folks, they kill their own also. But no, it means that raving lunatics that don't fear death and join what sounds a lot like a cult to me, were duped into giving their lives so that the person that told them to do it wouldn't have to. Now that I'm on that idea, maybe the following poem can illustrate my thoughts better than I'm describing.

Born On the Opposite Side

Let us never forget those who have fought and died for our country
Let us never forget to honor the families of those who have lost
Let us give praise and medals for winning the wars
And let us take the lives who were trying to take ours

But I beg you to consider that we should also never forget
That those we killed also died defending their country
That every man and woman deserves a proper service
That they were trying to take our lives because we tried to take theirs

While in Iraq I saw a lot of messed up shit. I saw starving kids with blisters on their feet from having no shoes, that were forced to beg for food and water, and we weren't allowed to do anything about it. I saw at least a thousand Iraqi men and women walk up to me to thank us for liberating them from a corrupt dictator. On one occasion, I had an Iraqi interpreter throw me down on the ground and throw himself on top of me to protect me from an RPG (rocket propelled grenade) that almost hit us.

Unfortunately, I was also shot at multiple times, and mortared regularly, by the very same countrymen.

But throughout everything I always told myself:

The people that are attacking us are ignorant, fanatical, and dangerous. It's not the entire country.

On April 19th, 1995 there was a man who destroyed the Alfred P. Murrah Building in Oklahoma City. When it happened, everyone knew it was an Islamic terrorist that had done it. The police searched for him and when they found him, it turned out it was a disgruntled former Army soldier. His actual name was Timothy McVeigh. That doesn't sound very Muslim to me.

Everyone was so quick to judge and already decided he was a Muslim terrorist. They also had no problem because it gave them the ability to blame another religion that was contrary to their own, rather than waiting and evaluating the facts. This must be a very human characteristic that we are innate with because it seems people do it without thinking; it's almost as if it was as natural as putting your keys in the ignition or putting your pants on one leg at a time. I'm going to wind up this chapter with a poem that can perhaps better explain exactly what I am trying to say.

I Saw A Terrorist

I once asked a man what a terrorist looks like
What I heard in response was tragically profound
A narrow mind projecting uneducated perception
I felt like the world had let this man down
A part of me wondered if society had failed
And I also thought the media was to blame
As it seemed his views were all slanted and skewed
And gave permission to label any and all the same
The obvious answers were the first to be thrown
A disgusting misuse of the stereotype
"An Arab, a Muslim", and the most notorious
"Any of the pilots from the 9/11 flights"
So I asked him who was to blame for Oklahoma City
And from which nation the Uni-Bomber hailed
Were McVeigh and Kaczinsky not considered germane
Because Timothy and Theodore are not Muslim names
If you want to know what a terrorist looks like
You need only to look to your left and right
Because terrorism is not bound by race or religion
It is defined by the actions of cowards that hide

Moral of the story: Being Islamic is not the same thing as being a terrorist.

CHAPTER 24

Religious? Spiritual? Extremist?

(Which One Are You?)

Let's talk about the difference between a spiritual person and a religious person for a moment, shall we? A religious person is one that takes their small beliefs and quickly takes it to a bad place, organized religion. I'm sorry, but I just can't think of a more appropriate way to word that at the moment. Again, that's subjective and my opinion only.

A religious person can't wait for the chance to put everyone that disagrees with them on trial and tell them "THIS IS THE ONLY TRUTH!!!" They're more prone to giving you lectures about why you're wrong and might even do everything in their power to get you to join their faith and find the "truth". Generally, it's probably because they care. I think they're either hallucinating on some good drugs, or they're just completely delusional. But that's me. In short, a religious person is bound by the rules of their religion, and they strictly abide by them.

A Jehovah's Witness for example is a religious person. The Jehovah's Witnesses are the ones that come to your doorstep and try to get you to join their local Kingdom Hall. I just threw that in there in case you've ever seen a Kingdom Hall and wondered what religion it belonged to. They ask you if you've heard the "good news". But when you come knocking on my door at 7 am the only news I'm classifying as "good" is you telling me you're going to leave and come back around 10 am after I've had time to eat my breakfast and wake up. The other sure-fire-way to spot a Jehovah's Witness is if you see them holding a copy of *The Watchtower*. They believe without question that only a few, 144,000 to be exact, along with a separate group known as the "great multitude" of men and women will be allowed to enjoy the splendor of Heaven. Everyone else that has died before Armageddon is just hanging out in purgatory and waiting to roast. That's one type of religious person.

Religious **extremists** love to take shit too far. That's why we call them "extremists". Whether it be violently screaming obscenities, physically attacking others, or even going as far as mass genocide, it's wrong. When you've reached the point of taking action against others, I feel you have overstepped your boundaries. There's no reason to intrude on someone else' life just because you have a different opinion.

Let's pick a controversial subject to use for an example. Take abortion for instance. I personally strongly disagree with abortion. I do however feel there are certain circumstances that should dictate the need for such an operation. Me personally, it's more a matter of the risk to the mother, how far along the baby is, and the fact that I think people need to be more responsible over their actions. If you are going to get pregnant or get someone else pregnant just because you were lazy, it's time to step up to the plate and start taking responsibility for your own actions. But in the end, it is a person's right to choose. Just as it is their right to choose whether or not to believe in God or be right or left-wing politically.

But since we're on the controversial subject of abortion, here are some facts to help justify my ideas of hypocrisy on murdering those who murder.

On July 29, 1994 Dr. John Britton and James Barrett were both shot to death outside of their abortion clinic in Pensacola, Florida. 'The good reverend' Paul Jennings Hill was charged with the murders. Yeah, again, that doesn't really make any sense to me. Killing other people for what you believe even though it had no effect on your life or liberties.

May 31, 2009: Dr. George Tiller was shot and killed by Scott Roeder as Tiller served as an usher at church in Wichita, Kansas.

On March 10, 1993, Dr. David Gunn of Pensacola, Florida was shot to death in the middle of an abortion protest by Michael F. Griffin.

The list goes on and on, but I think you can grasp what I am trying to state here. I have had this debate on more than one occasion with an anti-abortionist, and I almost always receive the same response. "Well, those people were just doing God's work for him". Then there's the one I hate the most, "Well, maybe those people believe that the Bible says an 'eye for an eye'". My response to that statement is usually, "Eye for an eye? Well, then you're an idiot because that's not an eye for an eye. An eye for an eye would be an abortionist doctor killing your child, and you, in turn, killing his child. That's an eye for an eye. What you are doing is called making yourself feel better. That's it."

What if everyone walked around and did things that made themselves feel better? Can you imagine that shit? We would have to start executing people for speeding tickets because all of our prisons would be overflowing with people arrested for acting on what made them feel better. Oh my God . . . . The world would be one giant state of Texas.

Is it really anyone's right to end someone else' life? If there even was a god that I believed in, I know he would not condone the merciless killing of innocent people. Perhaps these anti-abortionists would like to go around killing all of the Atheists and non-Christians too? And why stop there? While we're at it, we can kill the Jews, the Muslims, the Buddhists, and the Hindus, and have a modern-day Holocaust on our hands. And hey, with social networking, everybody will be able to "Tweet" about who they've just finished killing. That way if the person that's been murdered was one of your friends on FaceBook, you will know if you need to delete them from your friends list.

Why would anyone think that they have the right to pass judgment on anyone else, and then turn around and state that "Only God can judge me"? If I stay on this particular subject any longer, I am afraid this book will detour from my original intention. Let's get back to the difference between a spiritual person and a religious person.

A spiritual person is more likely to maintain good morals and try to live a pretty good life. They mind their elders, they pay their taxes, raise their children as best as they honestly can, and maybe even say grace at the dinner table. This kind of person most likely believes that God is not one to make you burn if you maintain a decent relationship with him and try not to do anything "bad" while you're on the Earth.

As a final thought to wrap up this chapter, I'd like to note the fact that spiritual people are also usually more open-minded to listening and actually hearing what someone has to say. They might have a line that they draw if it violates what they know is wrong. But everyone should have that line. I even have that line. They're usually not one to interfere with the affairs of other people's choices so long as the choices don't interfere with theirs. So, to the spiritual people out in the world, thank you for being genuinely good-hearted, and not being an extreme douche-bag.

Moral of the story: (Refer back to the title of this chapter)

CHAPTER 25

I Love the Bible

(It's the Best-Selling Novel of All Time)

I'm now going to begin dissecting some of the stories from the Bible. Some of the more common and argumentative stories in the Bible are Sodom and Gomorrah and the Tower of Babel. Sodom and Gomorrah were destroyed by the "wrath of God" correct? Abraham's nephew Lot tried to talk God out of the destruction of the city, and God agreed as long as Lot could bring Him 10 or so decent people from the city.

Upon returning to the city to search for some pure souls, Lot couldn't find any. Some "guests" show up who are actually angels sent from God to destroy the city and tell Lot to get the hell out of Dodge with his family. Lot was also instructed to not look at the city while it was being destroyed, and he listened. His wife didn't however, and she turned into a pillar of salt. That's the short version.

Devastating isn't it? Well here's how I see it. Apparently no one believes in earthquakes and volcanoes. Or perhaps even a meteor large enough to destroy a city. At the time of Sodom and Gomorrah, which I do think existed; everything extraordinary that happened was at the will of God. Sounds like the very same thing that the Greeks, Romans and Egyptians did; they asked permission for everything they did and offered praise for everything they had.

Why is it so hard to believe that a volcano could have erupted or a meteor could have crashed? God rained down fire and brimstone. But there is no way that volcanoes and meteors do the same thing right? Also, if you do your research you will find that the area where Sodom and Gomorrah are believed to be has hundreds of pillars of salt.

Surely, Lot's wife couldn't have been hit with fire and brimstone and toasted. I am not saying that you shouldn't believe what you want to believe; by all means, please do so. I'm simply saying don't be so quick to just shut out other people's ideas because they contradict your own. If you don't agree with something, ask about it. Give that person a reason why you believe what you believe. Be cordial and courteous to others and listen to what they have to say.

No matter what, don't turn it into a religious screaming match. One in which you are right, they are wrong, and that's all there is to it. "Yeah, now let's battle to the death to prove our loyalty to our faith."

I mean, that's one option. You could also try being open-minded and reserving your judgment until the end of the discussion. If you think that I am going to burn in Hell for writing this and believing what I believe, great! Just don't come to my house screaming at me for not agreeing with you. But I do encourage you to send me all of your hate mail. It's a great way for me to prove that my ideas are correct. Where was I?

The people who were in charge of writing the Book of Genesis (because I have difficulty believing Moses wrote all of it) probably witnessed the fire and the destruction that followed. Suddenly, it was "God" who did it. That is exactly the same as the Greeks claiming if they lost in battle it was because the gods didn't favor their victory. So I suppose every earthquake, tsunami, and volcanic eruption that happens throughout history is at God's will. But wait, there's a problem with that.

Theological determinism tells us that God is responsible for everything. He is in control at all times. But if God also gave mankind free will, the ability to make choices for ourselves, is He really in control of everything? I know that while I'm writing this, it is by my own choice and not by any sort of prophetic determination. So if that is true, exactly what year did God up and decide to step out of the limelight of destroying cities like Sodom and Gomorrah or flooding the Earth and killing all of humanity? Please tell me because that's probably an important part of history, and I want to have my facts straight.

Unless I'm mistaken there has never been any proof of His existence. All we have are stories and moral guidelines. When was the last time God stuck His head down from the clouds and was like, "Hey! You guys better knock that shit off! I mean it. I'm going to rain down the wrath of **ME** if you don't start getting your act together".

Every one of the stories in the Bible that demonstrates the wrath of God and all His might strike me as a bit odd and quite hypocritical. I cease to believe that an all-loving God would kill millions of people, on more than one occasion, for disobeying His commands; then turn around and offer you the key to the gates of Heaven. Do as I say, not as I do right? It's that kind of bullshit that bothers me.

You want to know what I think. I think it sounds a lot like the stories that we all tell our children in order to make them behave better. Except at the end of a children's story, there's a moral lesson to be learned. If you're bad as an adult, the only lesson we apparently learn is that you get to spend an eternity having your body ripped apart and have your flesh scorched off of whatever remains. And for all eternity?

"If you're not good then Santa Claus won't bring you any presents." It's the exact same, whether you want to admit it or not. The idea that these stories help to frame young minds into making the correct choices in life is a great tool for shaping morality in our youth. But at some point, you just have to cut the damn umbilical cord.

For me, there is no question about God's non-existence. It's what I believe, and my right to do so. As for adults who are very religious, you do not dare question the almighty power of the Lord, what He did, or anything that contradicts what you were raised to believe. You believe without question, end of story. And do you know what? There is nothing wrong with that as long as you are one of the righteous believers and not a phony. But you've got to get educated and get your facts straight people. You have to be able to know what you're talking about if you're going to talk about it.

I would like to touch briefly on the ideas of Heaven and Hell, before we get back to discussing God's wrath. I cannot justifiably imagine a world where you can do anything you want and go to the same place as the rapists, murderers, and child molesters. I love the idea of Heaven. Who wouldn't? It sounds like a great place, and you get to live there for eternity once you get through the gates. On that note, allow me to include some of my thoughts on the idea of Heaven and Hell.

Alex P. Hewing

What I Will Leave Behind

I am not afraid to take the next step
For I am no longer blind
And I will leave with no regrets
Of what I will leave behind.
I will walk with those from before
And be welcomed with arms opened wide
And will have no sorrow left on this earth
Of what I will leave behind
In front of me lie streets of gold
I need not worry of what was mine
And the riches that wait are far more great
Than what I will leave behind
My sole regret is sad to say
Were those that I loved through time
And I pray cry not for me today
To those I will leave behind

A Place To Be Feared

There is a place to be feared by all
Where all that can be seen is fire
Where the souls of the fallen are punished
For giving in to human desire
There is a place to be feared by all
Where pain and suffering are all you can find
Where the fallen angel reigns on high
And the slaves of his prison reside
There is a place to be feared by all
Where tears shall find no sympathy
Where your screams will cry a deafening mute
As the notes of a symphony

We are taught that there is a place to go for those who are either welcomed into the arms of the King of Kings for their righteousness, or a place to go for those who were naughty little boys and girls and were just never really able to kick the habit when they grew up. So who gets in there (Heaven), and what do we have to do in order to get in there? There are so many religions that have their own ideas of what constitutes someone's acceptance into Heaven. There are even huge discrepancies among the Christian denominations.

Getting back to the wrath of God, let's talk about the Tower of Babel. This is another great story from the Bible that I love to read. Located in the place that they called Babylon (presently Iraq, by the way), God reached out His angry hand again and destroyed all that inhabited the land. And for good reason too. Because man defied His word after He told them not to. Shame . . . . Shame . . . Shame . . . . I mean that goes back to The Ten Commandments. If you believe in the story, the city was supposed to build a great tower to honor God, but instead they built the tower for themselves as a demonstration of the achievement of man and all of their knowledge. Drawing attention from the Lord and worshiping themselves was breaking The Second Commandment. Now, that's day one stuff.

It goes on in the Book of Genesis to say that the people built a tower that reached to the heavens. Now if we're told to believe anything the Bible tells us because it is the word of God, you're saying that they built a tower that was so tall it actually ended up in the heavens. For anyone arguing that we can't take the translation literal I have one question for you: Which sections do we take as the truth? Let's take a look at some actual scripture shall we?

2 Timothy 3:

15 ". . . the holy scriptures, which are able to make thee wise unto salvation through faith which is in Christ Jesus."
16 "All scripture is given by inspiration of God, and is profitable for doctrine, for reproof, for correction, for instruction in righteousness."

In case you can't understand Biblical lingo, that scripture alone says that we are meant to take the Bible as the truth. That's almost impossible to do. I mean come on, if there was a certain height at which we could reach Heaven, we would have already done it. It would be more like a resort where people can vacation and then get back to their ordinary lives. A little farfetched I am sure, but no more than saying there is a tower to Heaven.

The fact remains that information can get distorted as it gets passed down generation to generation. You ever play the telephone game where one person starts a message on one side of the room and by the time it gets to the other side, it has completely changed from its original idea. That's what I'm talking about. Distorted truth. You can't say that the Bible is completely true and then dictate parts that are misinterpreted and mean something else. Here. Maybe this example will help illustrate my point better.

1st Generation
Jesus Christ is our Lord and savior. When the time comes, pass the message along to your son.
2nd Generation
Jesus Christ can't afford a Life Saver. When the time comes, pass the message along to your son.
3rd Generation
He beats his wife with a light saber. When the time comes, pass the message along to your son.
4th Generation
??????? . . . ???????

Why don't we look at it from a different perspective? We'll use Bob from 3rd Street again. Bob sees the Tower of Babel is so tall that it is well into the clouds. The next thing you know, some sort of natural disaster destroys it. He makes the claim that it was destroyed at the hand of God, and everyone believes him. I'm not saying in any way that is what happened; it's just an example. Time goes on and Bob's story ends up distorted in the Bible thousands of years later. Quite frankly, if the Bible is home to both truths and lies, it's pretty messed up because it's not fair to the billions of people that have put their faith in it. I do think that there are parts of the Bible that are true. Jesus Christ for example. I absolutely think he existed. I just don't think he woke up and went to Heaven three days after he was crucified.

Real quick while I'm thinking about it, we're told to obey man's law as well as God's laws. However, murder in the eyes of the lord is just as bad as making yourself an idol or coveting thy neighbor's wife (wanting to bang the MILF next door). I may not know everything about the justice system, but I do know that the men incarcerated in America's prisons for murder tend to serve a longer sentence than those who say "God Damn You". It goes without saying that killing someone is far more of a crime than cursing. So yeah . . . . figure that one out for yourself.

Please understand that I mean no harm in any of my rants. That is the last thing that I want. The whole purpose of this book is to get people to think a little more clearly and perhaps try to respect and understand each other a little better. I can't help but poke fun all day with funny quotes like this one that got me to laugh:

"Believing in God and Heaven because of what you read in the Bible is like believing in Hogwarts because you read a *Harry Potter* book." (Unknown)

I wonder how many religious fanatics I just pissed off? But if you stop and think about it, it's difficult to debate against. I really wish I could find the person that wrote this so that I can shake their hand and tell them thank you. I use that direct quote all the time. Actually, you know what? If I ever get the chance to meet the person that wrote that, I'm taking them out for a nice dinner at, like . . . . I don't know . . . . McDonald's or something, 'cause that's really all I can afford, but it's the thought that counts, I guess.

Logically, as far as evidence is concerned, there isn't a huge difference. Bring a *Harry Potter* book to a primitive race or even an indigenous people that are ignorant of the ways of the world, and see how many people you can get to believe there is actually a Hogwarts and a real Harry Potter. The only people who are really getting mad right now are the ones who can't argue my point with anything that can be considered substantial and not circumstantial.

Christians are told that the Bible is the devout truth. My question to that is . . . . which interpretation? The Bible has been revised a dozen times in dozens of languages for over 500 years. The first printed Bible was the Gutenburg Bible in the 1450's. For that matter, how one interprets the scripture can completely change the context and the message. An example:

Jeremiah 48:10—"Cursed is he who does the work of the lord deceitfully; cursed is he who keeps his sword back from blood."

Is this talking about people doing God's bidding by killing and persecuting others for not following their weak-ass translation of the Bible? That is how I interpret this scripture. But no, that is not what it actually means. However, that was my initial thought when I read it. I use this particular scripture only to illustrate my point.

Men and women have spent thousands of years arguing, fighting, killing, and persecuting over misinterpretation. Again, I make reference to "Bob from Third Street". He was told something wrong, or he told something wrong because he was crazy or a liar and got people to follow him. That brings to mind a good point I have wanted to touch on, another form of religious grouping called a cult. I am only going to mention it briefly, don't worry.

Cult—a specific system of religious worship, especially with reference to its rites and deity; a sect devoted to such a system; a quasi-religious organization using devious psychological techniques to gain and control adherents.

Sounds to me like a really good definition of a whole lot of today's religions. That third definition really defines the Catholic Church in my eyes. And that is just my point of view, and obviously not the views of the other 1/6 of the Earth that is Catholic, I am sure. My point is interpretation. I view the definition of a cult very closely related to many of the modern day religions in the world. Let's take a look at the definition of the word religion, shall we?

Religion: a set of beliefs concerning the cause, nature, and purpose of the universe, especially when considered as the creation of a superhuman agency or agencies, usually involving devotional and ritual observances, and often containing a moral code governing the conduct of human affairs.

Now, to me this definition sounds a lot more like a system of government than the definition of a religion. Maybe it's just because they are so closely related in their ideas. Both ideas center on control under a systematic body or individual that governs a group of people under specific rules. In my definition the only difference is I didn't add the part about the creation of a superhuman and the purpose and origin of the universe. Other than that, they are almost the same.

Moral of the story: There's nothing wrong with enjoying a book. But remember, there's a lot of books out there, and you can't believe all of them so why would you devote yourself to only believing one?

CHAPTER 26

I'm Definitely Going To Hell

Disclaimer: OK people, here's your full disclosure. I am about to upset some people. Probably, mostly Catholics, but maybe some other people too. Please try to remember that I mean no disrespect to anyone, and I aim to educate and entertain rather than alter anyone's beliefs. That being said, if you don't want to hear the truth because the truth hurts, you should stop reading right now. Yes, I am going to include my own opinions mixed in with some caustic, crude humor like I always do and there is nothing wrong with disagreeing with my opinion. I am also going to include a lot of facts. And forgive me for thinking this, but people seem to get more pissed off at the actual facts that I write about as opposed to my smartass opinions on different issues. But remember kids, it's better to be a smartass than a dumbass. So, let's get the hate mail started shall we?

Believe it or not, all sarcasm aside, I actually take a functionalist perspective on most social problems. This means that I don't look at social problems with a sense of placing blame on any one person or group. Instead, I look at the problem, evaluate the facts as to how the different variables interact with one another, and determine the best way for a solution to be reached. Granted, that sounds a little too textbook for most. All that it means is I try to remain unbiased and work with facts when trying to solve problems. Objectivity.

As previously mentioned, the Catholic faith is the largest of the Christian faiths, represented by over one billion followers. The Catholic adherents of the world make up over one half of the population that calls itself Christian.

Yeah, Catholicism is definitely the largest shareholder in the Christian business. Speaking of the Christian business, I tried to report the Catholic Church to the Better Business Bureau, but they were already on their list. HA!!!!! Did you see that? There's that crude humor that I mentioned before.

There are several issues and ideas from the Catholic Church that I am going to discuss. And by the way, for anyone thinking that I hate the Catholic faith, you can put that crap to rest right now. I do not hate any religion. Just because I don't agree with many of their policies, outlooks, and practices does not mean I hate them. I was enlightened when I first began reading about the Catholic faith to discover that the word Catholic simply means universal, which is why it is often correlated or replaced with the word ecumenical.

The Catholic faith follows several guidelines and rules, most of which are considered divine doctrine. It follows the majority of the 10 Commandments from the Old Testament as the other Christian denominations. That's not to say the Catholic Church doesn't have its own defining lines represented by their individual repetitive practices. First and foremost, the Catholic faith regards the Virgin Mary as a separate and almost equal deity, comparable to Jesus of Nazareth. They created what are known as the "Seven Deadly Sins", and the Catholics have their own Chief Commandments, or laws, of the Catholic Church.

Here are some examples:

If you are a true Catholic you are required to assist at Mass on Sundays and all holy days.

You have to fast on designated days.

You have to confess your sins at least once a year.

Take in the Holy Communion during Easter.

You have to support the Church; and

You must obey the laws of the Church in regards to marriage.

Catholicism was not always centered on the Roman Catholic Church that we know today. The main reason for this is because prior to Eastern Orthodox religions and the Protestant Reformation, Catholicism was amalgamated under the Christian followers all around the world. For the first 1,000 years of Christianity, if you belonged to any religion other than Christianity you were a heretic or you were viewed as a Pagan. You did not want to be a Pagan. Islam was rising up rapidly at that time from the 8th through the 11th century. This quickly led to the previously mentioned Crusades. That's all bullshit though. Money and power. Cash and control. That's all it was. To the men fighting the wars and dying for God/Allah, yes it was a religious war for the Holy Lands. But for the men on the throne, it was simply money and power.

Here's a little history on Catholicism for you.

1. Catholicism was originally a persecuted faith for approximately 300 years.
2. Catholicism remained as a persecuted faith until after Emperor Constantine's baptism and the organization of the Council of Nicaea.
3. The Roman Catholic Church follows the teachings of the apostles.
4. St. Peter whom is held to an extremely high regard is almost treated as a deity himself, the way the Virgin Mary is deified.
5. Every pope is believed to be the next spiritual successor after St. Peter beginning with Pope Leo I from the year 440-461A.D.

Like I said from the beginning, you can look all of this information up online. But I'd like to hone in on the pope for just a second. The Pope is elected to his position as the vicar, or messenger, of God. So . . . I'm guessing after he is elected and has his name pulled out of the magic hat, he is reborn spiritually and suddenly has God's personal cell phone number, right? The Pope is treated as the next closest thing to God himself for Catholics. Yet, the day before he is **ELECTED**, he is just another cardinal among the council at the Vatican. Hmmm . . . . ? Interesting? Moving on.

The Pope only serves one important role to the Catholic faith that I can sincerely agree with or at least understand. He is held to such a prestigious level and resides over the Catholic Church and its members so that in the event of an uprising, another Reformation, or any other dispute that may cause the Catholic faith to break apart, his word is the final word and is unquestionable. That is known as "ex cathedra", or quite literally, "from the seat of St Peter". It's more commonly referred to as papal infallibility. The only one that Christians are supposed to refer to as infallible is God. That's why I say the pope is viewed as the closest thing to God, Himself. I'm just stating facts. Seriously though, the Pope serves as a means of continuity for the entire Catholic faith and ensures that the principles of the apostles are carried on through time. Because his word is unchallengeable it allows the church to survive and thrive the way it does.

There are a few other variations in Catholicism that are not practiced or believed by the other Christian denominations. For example, Catholics believe in the idea of purgatory, the place we go and hang out while God decides if we did too many bad things while we were alive. Purgatory of course gave the Catholics a great window of opportunity in reference to the idea of indulgences.

For anyone who didn't know, indulgences were the Catholic Church's version of unnecessary fund raising. The idea basically states that family members who had lost their loved ones (usually nobility because they were rich and the church could get more money out of them) could pay the church to bring the deceased loved ones from purgatory to Heaven. If you couldn't afford it, they just sat in purgatory until you could. Essentially you are buying your loved ones way into Heaven. This particular idea was one of the main arguments brought to the Catholic Church's doorstep (and I do literally mean doorstep) by Martin Luther, which began the Protestant Reformation.

If you're raising your eyebrows at that in disbelief, you shouldn't, and here's why. It's really not much different than a certain Egyptian practice of filling a sarcophagus with treasures, artifacts, and other mundane items as a way to aid the dead on their long journey through the underworld. Then again, if you think the Egyptian practice sounds ridiculous and not the idea of indulgences because it's a Catholic practice, you need to take a look in the mirror. Most Christian denominations have a tithe of some sort.

Tithe—a tenth of one's income contributed voluntarily or as a tax to a charity or a church.

Another fact separating the Catholics from many other religions is that they believe in the idea of transubstantiation—the idea that the bread that is used in the Eucharist instantly becomes the body of Christ as soon as it is blessed by a priest. Other small variants between Protestant practices and Catholic practices include deutero-canonical books that were not recognized under other Christian denominations; the use of the crucifix and the rosary in prayers; the vows of chastity made by the clergy of the Catholic Church; and of course the monotonous veneration of the Catholic Saints, all 63,000,000 of them.

Now, since we're on the subject of Catholic Saints, here are my top 10 favorite patron saints that I found. Note: You will probably laugh at some of these, but I can assure you they are all 100% legitimate.

#10) If you suffer from narcolepsy you can pray to Saint Vitus, the Patron Saint of Oversleeping.

#9) Do you own a ferule? {<u>Ferule</u>: a baton, cane, or stick used in punishing kids} Perhaps you should pray to Saint Matilda, the Patron Saint of Misbehaving Children.

#8) Feeling bad about not tipping your cabby? Well you can relax and relieve yourself of your sins by praying to Madonna Della Strada (Our Lady of the Street), the patron saint of Rome's street sweepers and taxi drivers. Yes, it is real.

#7) Trying to land the leading role in the next big Hollywood blockbuster? No problem. Just take a moment to pay homage to Saint Genesius or Saint Vitus, the Patron Saints of Actors.

#6) Are you currently under court order to attend anger management therapy? Ask the judge if you can just take a moment to pray to Saint Jerome, the Patron Saint Against Anger.

#5) If you're confused about the justification of killing during wartime, you can consult Saint Barbara, the Patron Saint Against Death by Artillery.

#4) Suffering from a nasty spider bite during your vacation in Italy? Well rest easy knowing you can pray to get better soon through Saint Mark the Evangelist, the Patron Saint of Insect Bites and the Patron Saint of Venice. OK now, seriously? It's not enough to be the patron saint over all of goddamn Venice? No, you really needed to be the Patron Saint of Insect Bites too?

#3) If you happen to be preparing for the police exam and you need that extra boost, you can call on Saint Michael the Archangel, the Patron Saint of Police Officers.

#2) Downloading too much internet porn? Make sure and pray to Saint Isidore of Seville, the proposed Patron Saint of Internet Users and ask for his aid in redeeming your ways as a compulsive masturbator.

And coming in at 1ˢᵗ place is . . . . drum roll please . . . .

#1) Saint Paul the Apostle, the Patron Saint of Writers and Public Relations. The only freakin' patron saint I would ever pray to, if I did believe in God, in the hopes that it would have a positive effect on the number of copies that this book will sell.

If you didn't laugh at any of those it's probably just because you don't possess an anus or a sense of humor. Anyway, now that I've pissed off every practicing and non-practicing Catholic alike that thinks my humor is in poor taste, let's get back to the matter at hand shall we?

Now if you were upset from that last bit of information that was actually based on facts, you definitely do not want to continue on when I speak solely of my opinion of the Catholic Church.

About a week ago I was made aware of some emails that were circulating that I couldn't overlook. This next excerpt was taken from one of the emails that were written in the hopes that people like me would realize my decadent ways, and I guess just decide, all of a sudden, that Catholicism is the religion for me. The email was one of several that labeled me and every other Atheist as possessed by Satan and allowing Satan to act vicariously through me was some sort of massive, organized plan to turn those who believe in God into apostates.

It went on to be even more offensive by the author of the email signing the end of the message with "Your Loving Savior Jesus Christ". This was in an attempt to give the impression that God, or the Holy Spirit, was speaking through the author (Actually speaking through her hands and fingers as she typed). In reality it was nothing more than a sad, ostentatious attempt to rally others to her cause by using a figure as powerful as God as her spokesperson. Pay no attention to the lack of attention to the writing errors because God's infallible so we can overlook that one. But I'll let you read the email and make your own decision.

Message to Agnostics & Atheists
On November 18, 2010 @9:00 pm

"They are being guided by the demons. Some know that they are. Others don't. Pray that they see the truth before they continue on their futile path to emptiness. To the Atheists I say this. I love you no matter how you offend Me. To the Atheists who are being led and influenced by other beliefs stop and think. In their quest to follow manmade reasoning, they are simply following another faith. The belief that man is in control. He is not. Yet these same people, My precious children, for whom I will fight, are being encouraged to follow Satan, the Deceiver, and enemy of mankind. Ask the Atheist who goes to extraordinary lengths to pressurise (spelled incorrectly by the way) God's children why he does this. Is it not enough to simply deny me? Why do these people lie? Many of these Atheist groups have an agenda to entice and seduce My children into a false doctrine. Make no mistake their belief is another form of religion. A religion that exalts the power of intelligence, reason and pride. They emulate the very traits of Satan. They, in their blindness, follow another faith—the adulation of the dark where no love exists . . . "

"Can't you see that My word, My prophesy foretold so long ago may be the truth? Open your eyes and talk to Me once as follows: **God if you are the truth reveal to me the sign of your love. Open my heart to receive guidance. If you exist let me feel your love so I can see the truth. Pray for me now . . . ."**

"Your Loving Savior Jesus Christ"

I don't even know where to begin to explain how offensive this was, not just to me but also a few of my Christian peers that I showed the article to. It is a direct demonstration of religious persecution and a blatant exploitation of people's ignorance. And not only that, it's preposterous because it is written and signed by "God". Even the God-loving individuals that I showed this email to found it offensive and ridiculous. I do have to admit though, if there were a way to have God appear in the courtroom under subpoena we might be able to get the author on some incisive twist on plagiarism.

Moral of the story: Why in the Hell do we need a patron saint of Internet users? People, stop creating new idols to pray to. You're sinning and you don't even know it.

CHAPTER 27

The One and Only Commandment

(Don't Be An Ass)

The Ten Commandments are a really good topic to talk about; so let's tackle that right now. God first gave the Ten Commandments to Moses and told him to distribute His word to the people of Israel on Mt Sinai. Later, Moses was in charge of having the tablets placed into the sacred Ark of the Covenant, and blah, blah, blah. Time for some psychological and philosophical fun through the cunning use of satire.

The First Commandment: "I am the lord your God."

This commandment gives new meaning to the term "vague". At least it's pretty much the same in all Abrahamic and Judeo-Christian religions.

The Second Commandment: "Thou shall love no other god before me and thou shall not make yourself an idol." What this is saying is if you create another person or idol figure that is not God, you're breaking the Second Commandment, which is a sin. We can't say it's a major sin because we've all been told that every sin is the same in God's eyes. Just so we're clear, every idol figure we show interest in or follow is making us sin. Harry Potter and all of his followers are therefore spreading sin. Not to mention all of the Star Wars fans out there who think that the "force" is real and worship George Lucas. And if you want to be technical about it, worshiping the one and only Pope himself is, in a way, breaking the Second Commandment. I'm not looking for a debate on the matter. I don't care if you think that I'm wrong. I'm logical, and I know how to read. You can't just say it's a sin to make yourself an idol, and then be worshiped as the next closest thing to God Himself. But just in case, let's have a look at that word: i**dol: 1)** an image that is worshiped. **2)** one that is blindly adored.

Yep. That about sums it up for me. There is no doubt that the Catholics worship the Pope as an idol. And make no mistake people. I am not attacking the Catholics or the Pope. I am just using it as an example. If you take the scriptures word-for-word, the Pope is guilty of drawing attention away from God. Anyway, this commandment is the very reason the Tower of Babel was destroyed. If that is the case, then the creators of Star Wars, Harry Potter, and Simon Cowell are all Second Commandment breakers.

The Third Commandment: "You shall not make wrongful use of the name of the Lord your God." Once again in the eyes of God, one sin is as unforgiving as the next. Saying "goddamn" is just as bad as killing. This commandment is interesting because people misinterpret its meaning. Cursing is not the same as swearing. Taking the Lord's name in vain is sinning. Swear words are not considered taking the Lord's name in vain. Take the word "fuck" for example. Man created that word. There's no doubt about it. In fact, I am about 98.3% positive that wasn't around 5,000 years ago. For that matter, I don't know how many times I say the word goddamn in this book (I'm not even sure if I spelled goddamn correctly), but that is also breaking the Third Commandment because it is revered by most as blaspheming. Saying "goddamn you" is the most common form of blaspheming in my opinion. It violates the commandment because when you say it you are claiming that either God damned you or God is going to damn you, neither of which is the truth. Therefore, you are blaspheming. Goddamn, I am one perpetual sinner.

The Fourth Commandment: "Remember the Sabbath Day and keep it holy." For those that are unfamiliar, and I know so many people that are, Sunday was not the original Sabbath Day (God's Day). Saturday was the original Sabbath Day. That's also one of the main reasons the Jews didn't care much for Christ. Jesus Christ was performing miracles on Saturdays. Now let's consider the facts: Jesus was a Jew, and he was breaking the Fourth Commandment. It therefore stands to reason that they found discontent with him acting against God. I'm not saying; I'm just saying. That doesn't give them the right to put him to death. I'm just rationalizing some common misconceptions.

Come to think about it, most people attend religious services on Sunday and never on Saturday. That means, no matter what, all of these people are breaking the Fourth Commandment every week. Not only that, they're doing it in an organized fashion. Hmmmm???? Makes perfect sense. In all actuality, Christians presently use Sunday as the Sabbath Day in commemoration of the resurrection of Jesus Christ.

The Sabbath Day was initially meant to be the seventh day of the week. It's not like the Christian faiths actually think the Sabbath Day is Sunday. They just celebrate it on the first day of the week as opposed to the last day of the week, as it was originally supposed to be. There are obvious inadequacies surrounding the idea of determining the Sabbath Day. The rule is generally applied to the fact that God finished His creation of the heavens and the Earth on the sixth day and then he rested on the seventh day. Getting right down to it, you can sum it up to separating the Old Testament from the New Testament, or the Jewish faith from the Christian faith. I just really like to piss people off with philosophical arguments that debate every day hypocritical BS.

Now some might think this is the most easily followed and obeyed commandment. But wait . . . . how many people don't go to church on Saturday or Sunday? If you actually say you believe in this commandment, you're sinning. Tsk. Tsk. Tsk.

The Fifth Commandment: "Honor thy mother and father." We're told to honor the Lord through the obligation of our love for God. I don't really know how to delve too deep into this one except to say—look at any juvenile home and the fact that the children that are beaten and molested are expected to honor their parents. Kind of messed up, right? Can't blame the kids, and you can't break God's laws. And what about the children in orphanages? Do they only honor God and not their parents, because they don't know their parents? If they don't honor their parents because they haven't met them are they sinning? I'll let you be the judge.

The Sixth Commandment: "Thou shall not kill/murder." This one is a debate just waiting to be started. First of all, depending on which side of the fence you happen to be on, killing and murder are the same thing. Based solely on religious context, we're told that the ideas of killing vs. murder are separated by what we call bloodguilt, or the shedding of innocent blood. The Hebrew Bible, for example, also strictly prohibits unlawful killing, but justifies it if it relates to warfare, self-defense, or capital punishment (i.e. the death penalty). Should be cut and dry, right?

Here's a thought: According to the Bible we're not supposed to kill if it is considered the shedding of innocent blood. But we're also allowed to kill if it's in warfare, correct? So, for the millions of innocent people that are killed in times of war, in places like Hiroshima and Nagasaki, are their deaths considered murder or just killing. Keep in mind, we're talking about approximately 160,000 innocent men, women and children that woke up that day and have never done a thing to harm America. That's an important factor when trying to justify genocide. It's in a time of war, and we're talking about killing innocent people. I'm not judging. I'm asking you to reasonably justify murder vs. killing. You can probably leave it alone at one man's murder is another man's killing. The justification is left to someone's perception, much like every other commandment. Those goddamn commandments. Oops . . . . Just broke the fourth one again.

Note From the Author: **Anybody out there that is hating on me right now for saying that dropping nuclear bombs on Hiroshima and Nagasaki isn't considered genocide should read the fine print.**

genocide: n. the systematic annihilation of a political, racial, or cultural group.

All I know is 160,000 innocent Japanese being wiped out all at once, sounds like a systematic annihilation of a cultural group to me. Anybody else? Wasn't there another genocide going on at the same time? What was it? I can't remember. Oh, yeah. That's right. The Holocaust.

The Seventh Commandment: "Thou shall not commit adultery." America is just full of Seventh Commandment breakers, aren't we? Thanks to Bill Clinton, Thomas Jefferson, and John F. Kennedy, America even has devout Seventh Commandment breakers running the **country**. If America wants moral fiber, I don't think they should be listening to the 10 Commandments. I think they should be listening to 60's music, legalizing marijuana, handing out condoms with every high school and college text book that students finish, and attempting to do all of those at the same time.

Let me get back on track though. Adultery is another one of those perception-based commandments. Adultery is cheating on your spouse, point, blank, and period. I hate to put it so plainly, but in all fairness, it's a pretty good description. I'm not going to go into too much depth philosophically on this one.

I will say that this particular commandment is broken a lot more than people think, and I don't mean because men or women cheat on each other more often than not. If you really want to follow the commandments to the "T", unless your divorce is completely, 100% finalized with whatever state you filed for divorce, you're still technically married. That means, for all of the people in the world who begin dating and having sex with other people before their divorce is complete, they are all breaking the Seventh Commandment. But it's OK. Thanks to the technicality of divorce not even existing when the commandments were handed down from God, I guess this is one rule that was just destined to be broken.

The Eighth Commandment: "Thou shall not steal." There's not really a lot of room for argument on this one, sorry. It's wrong to steal. The only argument anyone could philosophically bring to the table isn't exactly a secret. Is it ever OK to steal? That's up to you. If my kids are starving and I don't have any money to buy them food, yeah, I'm probably going to steal the food. I'll spend one night in jail to keep my girls alive. They mean more to me than anything else in the world. But seeing as the last few commandments got so much attention, and because I want to make this one look important too, here's some fun facts (that have nothing to do with the 10 Commandments, by the way) for you to read while I use up some more white space in the book:

While serving the one year mandatory military service for all males in Austria, Arnold Schwarzenegger went AWOL during his basic training to compete in the Jr. Mr. Europe contest. He subsequently served one week in military prison.

Chuck Norris' actual name is Carlos Ray Norris. He acquired the nickname "Chuck" while serving in South Korea (and began training to become the baddest mother-fucker on the planet).

Coulrophobia is the fear of clowns (and probably wasn't even officially diagnosed until Stephen King wrote the book *It*).

The surface of the Sun is approximately 9,800 degrees Fahrenheit.

The circumference of the Earth is 24,906 miles, or 40,075 kilometers if you happen to somewhere other than the U.S. (because apparently the U.S. still refuses to get on board with the metric system).

The slang term "hooker", used in reference to prostitutes, was popularized by Civil War Major General Joseph Hooker, due to his illustrious parties and frequency of women that were common at his headquarters.

Kellogg's Corn Flakes was accidentally created when Dr. John Harvey Kellogg fed the patients from the Battle Creek Sanitarium in Michigan a batch of stale, pressed wheat rather than throw it away, in an effort to save money. The patients found it to be rather tasteful and enjoyed it.

The word racecar is spelled the same forwards and backwards.

58% of all facts and statistics are made up on the spot. (I know what you're thinking. "Is he making that up?")

The Ninth Commandment: "Thou shall not bear false witness against your neighbor." That means lying. This commandment, like almost all the others, is based almost entirely on perception. There are so many ways that someone could easily misunderstand this. Just for fun, let me throw a few more philosophical objections at you.

For one, what was considered lying 5,000 years ago is probably not considered lying today. Lying is considered bearing false witness, and bearing false witness is the same as saying something that is not true. What about when somebody says something that they thought was true, but later they found out was false? Are they breaking the Ninth Commandment? Or somebody that identifies a murderer from a lineup, that isn't the murderer. If that person is then sent to prison, under **FALSE** pretense, did the person that identified them lie?

Does cheating on your spouse count as two sins, since you committed adultery and lied to your spouse, by agreeing to be faithful to them when you got married? Is repeating the same lie over and over again counted as sinning repeatedly, or just once, because it was the same lie? Are pathological liars sent straight to Hell for making a public mockery of the Ninth Commandment? Seriously though, if access to Heaven was based on a total number of sins that were committed while on Earth, pathological liars are just fucked.

The Tenth Commandment: "Thou shall not covet thy neighbor." First of all, this one is also known to include coveting anything that belongs to your neighbor. Bringing the 10 Commandments to a close, this final commandment discusses God's declaration of being envious of your neighbor's possessions. And yes, I am of course going to throw a few last minute arguments in about it.

God's word is final. It is divine mandate. That's actually good news for us all. That means, we might not be able to desire our neighbor's belongings, but it's not the end of the world. Thanks to another loophole in the system, we can all just travel two streets down and get away with not sinning. Before you get too excited, yes, I am aware that "neighbor" refers to the fellowship of mankind, meaning everyone. But again, it's unfair to call something the truth verbatim, and then change the rules based on whatever your interpretation is at the time. It's just easier to call it what it really is, a really good guideline.

Just on a side note, I found it interesting that, in Exodus 20:17, God proclaimed that we're not allowed to covet our neighbor's wife, his ox, his donkey, his manservant, or anything else that belongs to our neighbor. I'm just curious. Isn't manservant another way of saying slave? If that's the case, then I am curious as to how He is **not** OK with you secretly desiring the things that belong to your neighbor. But He is totally fine with you owning a slave????? America's pledge of allegiance states, "One nation, under God . . . ." Perhaps the acceptance of slavery in the U.S. can be better explained by the fact that U.S. currency has "In God We Trust" stamped on it. I guess George Washington, Ben Franklin, and John Hancock figured, if God's OK with it, I guess we can be too.

Wrapping up this chapter, let me just say one more thing. The Ten Commandments are a great tool for building moral guidelines and principles for mankind. Stealing is wrong. Lying is wrong. Murder is wrong. It's amazing. We have laws against all of those. It's time for the world to accept the fact that the Ten Commandments were great building blocks to help mankind not destroy itself. They've done a good job too, for the most part. The world no longer needs Ten Commandments. Most people aren't following them anyway. The world has evolved. We're not following Hammurabi's Code anymore either for the same reason. It's over baby. It's time to let it go.

Moral of the story: The only commandment we should need to abide by is: Don't be an ass. I think that sums up all ten pretty well.

CHAPTER 28

Refer Back to Chapter 27

The very foundation of morality around the world is based on primitive laws of governing right and wrong. The 10 Commandments, the Code of Hammurabi, they're all doctrine designed to set up a uniformed set of laws or rules. But a law doesn't need to be present for someone to know murder is wrong. I think that's something that can be considered a general understanding. Again, there will always be special cases to argue against my point.

Think about how many laws are in place that millions of people disagree with. Dozens of bills are passed by Congress that the majority of the American population is none the wiser of. And let's not forget the fact that laws change with time. It wasn't always legal for African-Americans or American women to vote. In contrast, it wasn't always illegal to smoke marijuana in the U.S.

It doesn't just stop with man's laws either. God's laws have also changed, another fact that many religious idiots continue to remain oblivious of. As mankind's understanding has changed throughout history, so does our interpretation of constitutes right and wrong. What we read about in the Old and New Testament as right and wrong is completely different than what is considered right and wrong today.

The church, or more accurately illustrated, the men and women that worshiped God, had nowhere near the same governing laws 3,000 years ago. Ancient Sumerians didn't count eating meat on Friday as an act against God. Drug and alcohol abuse, sex crimes, and even driving an automobile (if you happen to be Amish), are all examples of actions that go against what different religions today say is right and wrong. With time, and, you guessed it, education, religions and governments have created new laws for mankind to live by.

Murder is not wrong because it goes against the 10 Commandments; it is wrong because it is wrong to unlawfully kill someone. The damage that is caused and the hurt that is felt from murder were still present before the 10 Commandments. Sex before marriage is not wrong. Sex with a child is wrong. Unprotected sex is wrong. A pregnant teenager with two kids that is forced to drop out of school and therefore negate any further education is wrong.

That's a good tangent to go off on. The more churches patronize kids today and parents coerce their children away from sex, the more today's youth is going to covet the idea. Parents should try talking to their kids. Let their uneducated minds understand the ramifications of their actions should they decide to have sex and to practice safe sex if they do decide. You can get a more positive result in character, maturity, and parent/child connection if you are real with your children.

It makes sense, and that is exactly the way you should explain it to them. Wait until you're an adult and out of school before you start having kids. Use protection to help prevent STDs, which there are more and more of every day it seems. This is not a current event people. We have known about it for a hundred years, and yet we are still making mistakes. For the men out there reading this, stop getting married just because you happened to get a girl pregnant; it almost always ends up bad. That doesn't mean to abandon your responsibilities. It actually means the opposite.

If you want to call yourself a man, MAN UP! Take care of your kids. Stop running away from your responsibility every time you are placed in a position that requires you to overcome adversity.

Ladies, quit getting pregnant because you think it will make a man stay with you. Do you realize where that road leads to? The man is either going to run like a coward, in which case you don't end up with him anyway, or he is going to resent you when he finds out you did it on purpose. That resentment, coupled with the exhaustion of a new baby, leads to constant arguing and fighting. The next thing you know, he's regretting staying with you and making you suffer for it by coming up with excuses for not spending time with you and always wanting to be out with his friends. The ultimate result of course being the two you either breaking up, or worse, getting divorced if you are married. Now your kids suffer because the two of you weren't responsible enough adults to think before you acted.

I'm certain there are a large number of people that would read this and think that I am attacking them personally (If they are guilty). However, my words are sincerely meant to edify anyone that would be open-minded enough to read this book and understand it for its intended purpose and not just a list of insults and finger-pointing.

I should probably state for the record that I got married when I was very young to my first wife whom I hardly knew. We have a beautiful daughter named Serenity, and the two of us managed to part on good terms which most divorcees can't say, save a few obscure situations. The two of us do our very best to make it as easy and healthy as we can on our daughter as possible. The problem of course is even though we're friends I'm still filled with a constant self-loathing of only getting to see my absolutely wonderful daughter every other weekend because of schedule conflicts. So before you start saying, "You don't know what you're talking about" let me be the first to tell you, I know exactly what I am talking about. Time for another Xanax!

Moral of the story: Anyone past a certain age is considered an adult. It takes responsibility of your actions to measure someone's maturity.

CHAPTER 29

In Your Name, I Pray . . . .

(Now That I've Just Prayed for My Acne to Clear Up, Maybe I Can Finally Get Laid)

Once upon a time, there was a man named Bob from Third Street who died and went to Hell. When he arrived the devil asked him how he died. The man said, "I was in a car accident and I died of internal bleeding while waiting for the ambulance to show up. But there's something I don't understand. I was praying to God, asking Him to come and save me, when I died. Why wasn't I saved?"

The devil replied by saying, "Perhaps you should have prayed for a faster ambulance. They probably could have done something to actually save your life."

I'm about to discuss the very controversial subject of God's power and the power of prayer. Two of the biggest questions that I debate with people are: What exactly is God in control of, and does God really answer prayers. Fundamentalists maintain the belief that God is responsible for everything. Such an example is explained by determinism. But everything? Really? So, when a football team prays before a game, and they win, it is because they prayed. But if the team loses, it's because they prayed and I guess God had already promised the other team dibs on winning the game. Or how about this one? When old people die, it is part of God's plan. However, when babies die . . . . it is part of God's plan. Hmmm? If you're hissing at me, I gave you fair warning that this whole book was very controversial. I grow more and more frustrated that I myself am guilty of spending the first 20 years of my life praying for everything bad to get fixed, rather than doing something about it myself.

All right then. How about a true story? One summer when I was a kid, I was away at church camp. I think I was around the age of . . . . It doesn't fuckin' matter. While at camp, I got an eye infection. The pastor and his clergy at camp came back to my cabin with eye drop antibiotics. They placed two drops in each eye as instructed on the label and then proceeded to pray for me to get better. Three days later, through the power of their prayers, the infection was gone. No, the infection was gone because of the medicine they put in my eyes for three days. If the infection had not gotten better, does that imply that God was busy that week? Was my church camp experience being ruined part of God's plan? Is God not the benevolent God I had heard and sang about every day at church camp? No? Oh, perhaps God didn't like Caucasian males named Alex? The answer is . . . None of the above.

Joking aside, this is only my personal view on the subject. I will not tell someone they are ridiculous for believing in prayer, UFOs, or anything else I just happen to disagree with. It would be unfair and hypocritical for me to do so. I do not have the right to pass judgment on anyone as long as their actions do not impede on my life or well-being.

My cousin Hoosname Duzzent Madder once told me that a woman in a hospital asked him to pray for her husband's recovery as he was told he had a slim chance of a successful survival through surgery. My cousin is a very God-loving man so he agreed to pray for her husband. The woman asked my cousin, "Do you think God will save my husband?" My cousin replied by saying, "I think he has the power to."

What a bullshit cop out! I love my cousin to death, but that answer was a bit cowardly and ambiguous. The idea that God is all-benevolent is slightly misleading considering he seems to pick and choose who to favor and help. If you're a person that trusts in prayer and you doubt what I'm saying, you should try jumping from an airplane without a parachute and ask God to save you. Studies have shown that gravity will beat God 100% time.

Moral of the story: If you want to save someone from falling from a cliff you should extend your actual hand to help them. Folding your hands and mumbling words will never offer the same results.

CHAPTER 30

Not Even an Honorable Mention

It's time to talk about some serious history. Has anybody out there ever tried out for a team and just didn't make the cut? Somebody decided the effort you put forth just wasn't quite what they were looking for. That must have been how all the authors of the books of the Apocrypha felt. The Apocrypha, for any who are unaware up until this point, is the collection of books that were not added to the various versions of the Bible because they were deemed apocryphal (which actually means "of questionable authorship").

For reasons such as negative or contradictory connotation against what the powers-that-be wanted, several books, by several different authors, were sadly never added to the Bible. And what exactly gives these few individuals the right to dictate what is truth and lies? If a man (other than the pope) came out today and publicly claimed he had consulted with God and was instructed to add his own book to the present day Holy Bible, he would be laughed at, ridiculed, and probably threatened by several extremist groups with acts of violence. But honestly, why is now so different from 1700 or so years ago?

We believe and support only certain individual first-person accounts. Those other idiots are either delusional, lying, or both. Right? Must be. Why else would one person's word be more accurate than another?

How many people out there believe in ghosts? Yeah, that's something we can look at similarly. If you went to the police and told them that your house was haunted, they would have to do everything in their power to not laugh at you. On the other hand, if you write a book about ghosts that you've seen with your own eyes and label it as "Based on a True Story", you'd be surprised how many people are stupid enough to believe it. Hell, a lot of them would probably begin to perpetuate facts they claimed to have looked up to other people, when in fact, they've never done one bit of research on their own, especially about ghosts.

How many people almost pissed themselves when they watched any of the *Paranormal Activity* films? Well, I don't know the exact number, but I'll bet it was a lot. I don't believe in ghosts, but my hair was standing on end through the whole last 20+ minutes of the movie. These first-person accounts in film and literature are all fictitious. Yet they constantly get people to believe that they're true, because the writers and directors put the words "Based on a True Story" on the movie. Do you know how many people tried to convince me that the film *The Blair Witch Project* was real, and the cast is still missing to this day? Those people are going around spreading lies that will probably end up being believed by other people, who will then spread the lies even further.

I think Stephen King is one of the creepiest fucking, best-selling authors I've ever seen. Have you seen that guy? He looks like he could star as a zombie in a movie . . . . without wearing any makeup.

Regardless of how ridiculous the story is, if Stephen King told everyone that he witnessed actual ghosts, aliens, God, or anything else, he would have a huge number of people believing it. We're talking about one person claiming they had an experience, first-hand, wrote a book about it, and got other people to believe them. It really isn't that much different than any of the books of the Bible, in all honesty. No one has ever proven that ghosts exist. Yet, look at how many people say that they believe in them.

I've got a little experiment I'm going to conduct right now, while you read this.

I have a friend named Johnny. I've known him for years. For the most part, Johnny is a very respectable, honest, and trustworthy guy. But there was one day in particular that I remember, when he made me question how much validity I placed in his words. A while back, he told me that he witnessed a guy communicating with people from beyond the grave (At that point, by the way, he had already almost lost me, but I let him continue). After that, he said he even witnessed this same guy bringing somebody back from the dead. As a good friend, I had to tell him how difficult it was to believe him, and that he should probably make an appointment with a therapist. How many people out there agree with me? For all of the people out there that raised your hand, you have obviously never read the Book of John.

Yes, I made up that whole story about my friend "Johnny", but here's why. In the Book of John, we're told of the power of Jesus being demonstrated through seven signs of divinity. The culmination of Jesus' seven signs was the resurrection of a man named Lazarus. Yeah, for all of you who said you don't believe in bringing people back from the dead, that one's for you. Resurrection = Bringing people back from the dead. If you believe the stories from the Book of John, but you don't believe anybody today that says they saw somebody bring a man back to life, you're a hypocrite.

The point is crystal clear. It's not fair to exclude the validity of one person's first-person account, just because it says something different than what you believe. If you're going to call some of the books "of questionable authorship", you'd better call all of the books "of questionable authorship".

While I realize it may be rather audacious of me to make radical accusations about the group that had the right to pick and choose what would be considered correct, it's also the truth. So I'll understand if it's difficult to come to grips with because the truth always is. If you are open-minded enough to do the research yourself upon reading this, please do. I am sure you will be enlightened to find that the accounts of authors such as Matthew, Mark, Luke, and John are just as provable as any of the dozens of books by the authors in the Apocrypha that were thrown out, like that loaf of bread that now has penicillin growing on it.

Here are some fun facts . . . .

1) Up until the King James Version, (the first one I mean) the Apocrypha was included in the Bible.
2) Some books of the Apocrypha are still included in the Catholic Bible. They are referred to as Deutero-canonical books, and they are not accepted by the majority of other Christian denominations.
3) Martin Luther made note of his doubts on the authenticity of four books in the New Testament, including: the Epistle to the Hebrews, the Epistle of James and Jude, as well as the Revelation of John.

It's ridiculous. If a book is written by man claiming to be the true word of God, it is apocryphal. The books in the Apocrypha were voted against and deemed non-canonical through hundreds of years of misinterpretation. Of questionable authorship? There is no question if you ask me. Mankind is capable of making mistakes and therefore we should all be taken as apocryphal authors. I mean, come on, at least the Baghavad Gita fell from the sky in the Hindu myths from the Mahabharata. So at least according to their myths it really did come from the sky. Granted that's still ridiculous, but at least they're claiming it really did come directly from their God and was not written by man.

Anyone that wants to can feel free to call me apathetic or even profoundly cynical if you want to. To those people I would say what I have already said a billion times before. I mean no disrespect to anyone. In fact, many of my friends today are either extremely religious or at least say they're Christian (even if the majority know nothing about their own faith). However, anyone that happens to be reading this and doesn't like what I have to say can just do what the majority of the rest of society does, which is stop reading. That's what the ignorant, intolerant, uneducated, sorry excuses of our society seem to do, and they are doing just fine. That is, if you don't count the embarrassing and unintelligent slant that they unfortunately label the rest of us with.

Moral of the story: Unless you can prove it, it will always be questionable.

CHAPTER 31

Creationism vs. Evolution

Visions of grandeur. That's what God must have had when He created the universe. Yes, God is truly a kind and just God. He must have been to be so kind as to place our planet's sun, the closest star in our solar system, at the exact point at which His beloved children could live and be prosperous. A real math wiz God is too. Placing the sun a little closer to Earth would have meant life was never possible because it would have been unable to survive the extreme heat caused by our planet's dissipated magnetosphere, which protects the Earth from solar radiation.

But there is another possibility. What if the planet started off without life on it for millions of years? Then the simplest forms of life such as bacteria could have begun growing. After a few billion years the planet would have more complex life forms on it including plant life. Time would have allowed the planet to cool down, change its atmospheres, and undergo weather changes that allow water to cover the Earth in the forms of oceans and seas. What would we actually call that? Oh yeah, that's called evolution. That's the other side of the coin.

I wonder how big the universe was when God first created it. Given the fact that the universe is ever-expanding, I wonder how far ahead God planned that out. I wonder how many people are completely unaware that the universe is in constant expansion. I wonder how many of those never bothered to look up any information on it because they were told to just believe without question. I wonder how many people never learn anything that contradicts what their parents or friends tell them? I wonder how many of them will go on being slaves, completely oblivious of everything real that surrounds them? I wonder?

I apologize if my questions seem too forward or direct. I was actually wondering about these questions as I wrote them. My mind was not able to fathom how people could be so blind as to not question ideas such as these and just go along with it for so long. But then it occurred to me. I was the exact same way about six years ago. People don't know any better, and they are always looking for answers to practically unanswerable questions. So, when they hear a story of how everything began, they accept it as truth because it filled the empty hole that was there before. It doesn't matter that the answer to the question was that God farted, and Venus was created.

I realize it can be difficult to come to grips with. Hell, it was for me too. But I also felt a huge weight lifted off of my shoulders from carrying all of these unanswerable questions my whole life. For me, science answered many of those questions. For the ones that it didn't answer, it gave answers that made the most sense to me. For you, everything about Islam, Hindu, Judaism, or Christianity may fill that void. For me though, I believe the Earth is very old and has evolved to its current state.

If you want to believe that God is responsible for the biological anomalies that we encounter throughout the universe, go right ahead as long as you truly believe it and know why you believe it. If it makes sense to you, go for it. Frankly, I don't care if you also believe in Santa Claus, the Easter Bunny, leprechauns, or unicorns either. That is your right, and I wouldn't dare tell you that you were wrong for believing it. I may be thinking of some funny things to say to you, but I would never lash out against you for having an opinion.

That being said, if you're not interested in basing your understanding of the world on facts, then Santa Claus, (the one that flies around with reindeer every Christmas) the Easter Bunny, leprechauns, and unicorns are just as easy to believe in as God. So please don't persecute anyone for believing in those either.

If you want to throw philosophical objections at me, go right ahead. I get it all the time with people telling me that I am a hypocrite for believing in evolution but not believing in divine creation because there is no proof of God's awesome power. I was not around, nor was anyone else, to witness the Earth and its millions of forms of life evolve. I wasn't there to see the Milky Way galaxy being born. I just put my faith in something that I can observe, test, and calculate in order to deduce my own beliefs.

Neither creationism nor "Big Bang" is provable. One of them is scientific and logical, while the other just says, "This is how it happened and just believe it because I'm not smart enough to understand concepts as large as this". They are both completely based on personal preference. By the way, I have to give it up to the scientific community for naming their theory on the creation of life after something that sounds like a sexual orgy.

Now that we're on a role with a scientific discussion, let's move on to every Sci-Fi dreamer's version of Heaven.

Moral of the story: It doesn't matter whether you believe in creationism or evolution. All that matters is that you pay your taxes every year so that the government doesn't repossess your house.

CHAPTER 32

Sci-Fi vs. Fantasy-Fiction

(Extra-Terrestrial Intervention vs. Divine Intervention)

Trekies, Star Wars fanatics, and the small population of Dr. Who fans that are still out there, lend me your ears. Ah yes, extra-terrestrials. Ohhh, where do I begin? In this chapter I will be discussing a few of the common theories believed by UFOlogists, science-fiction enthusiasts, and basement troglodytes.

Unfortunately, I'm not going to go into my ideas on the major UFO and extra-terrestrial conspiracy theories out there. Reason being is that it bares hardly any relevance to the thesis of this book. I'm already going off on quite a few tangents in this book that I shouldn't as it is. Perhaps that can be one of main ideas of one of my next books. By the way, if you haven't eaten in a while you may want to because I'm about to talk your ear off.

Space. There's a lot of it. Even with our advances in modern science and technology, we still can't see past of the edge of our nose, figuratively speaking of course. Why is it so difficult to believe that we are not the only ones in this universe? Forget all of the probabilities and statistics used to calculate the chances of life on other planets and just be realistic for a minute. We as humans would have to be incredibly naïve and vain to think that we were the only intelligent forms of life in the entire universe.

So why then is one more believable than the other? The truth is, neither of the ideas is more provable than the other. It is perfectly acceptable to claim that human beings are, as we have always been, made in God's image. So, why not the other? Anyway, my point is not to defend either side as to which is correct. My point is to emphasize the importance of being open-minded enough to listen to someone else' views without immediately judging them. Regardless of whether you're living in a fantasy-fiction world or suffering from science-fiction dementia, just because you disagree with what I believe doesn't mean we can't both tolerate one another.

Believe it or not, if you remove some of the "word for word" scripture, most people can see how alien beings could have been misinterpreted for God or gods. It also furthers the ideas that civilizations that don't understand something advanced, simply call it supernatural.

Many followers of extra-terrestrial intervention believe that the expression, "God made man in his own image" actually refers to an alien race that either visited Earth or actually lived here thousands of years ago and decided to give birth to a new race. This doesn't necessarily contradict the idea behind "God" creating man in His image. It just offers a more science-fictional approach to it. This theory, that is popular among the science-fiction genre of the world, explains why humans are so much alike in symmetry and physiology to the alien creatures that have been described for thousands of years.

The basic idea is that alien species that visited us created a new advanced life on Earth by placing their own DNA in creatures already living here. Such a notion answers one of the biggest unsolved mysteries of all time, the missing link. This ancient astronaut theory states that the link between early Cro-Magnon and perhaps Australopithecines made the evolutionary jump to intelligent life when an alien race placed its DNA in the human specimens. When this happened, the alien life forms passed some of their intelligence on to the current human race along with it.

In case you were wondering, I didn't make that last title up. Ancient astronaut theorist is the politically correct term E.T. enthusiasts (that believe in the ancient astronaut theory) call themselves to appear more professional to the general public and scientific community. Personally, I think that makes about as much sense as calling Scooby-Doo a canine-investigative reporter, but that's me. Anyway, assuming the alien race did intervene with human life, it worked. The evolutionary chain that could not explain how mankind went from grunting and flinging feces to suddenly and dramatically being able to create languages, buildings and whole civilizations now had an answer, maybe not a provable one, but an answer none-the-less.

There are differences of opinion when discussing the reason behind extra-terrestrial intervention such as the alien race wanting to ensure its survival genetically. But probably the most widely accepted and popular idea is that the alien race wanted to do what so many of today's humans are trying to do. They wanted to play God. And in case you're wondering, yes this whole theory implies that every human shares a chromosome or two with the alien species that created us. Difficult to believe? Yes. Provable? No. Possible? Definitely! Which is why this idea is just as believable as any other religion and deserves no persecution for believing it.

Countless religions throughout time have artistic depictions and written descriptions of alien beings and what the modern-day world calls UFOs. It pretty much just goes back to the idea of a culture or population not possessing the knowledge or education to interpret extra-terrestrials as anything but gods because they didn't have the technology to explain it in any other way. There are a lot of reasons why so many ancient astronaut theorists believe what they do. For example:

The Hindu faith has stories in its religious texts describing great battles of creatures from the sky coming down to the Earth and waging war with the human race and each other. The Chinese have almost the same stories. The Chinese also have stories that describe the body of a man being taken over by a being from the sky, thus giving the human supernatural powers. Sounds an awful lot like a modern-day deification to me. But that's not even the beginning of the similarities to these unexplainable aliens/gods.

For anyone that holds a strong foundation of Christianity, allow me to pull an actual excerpt from the Bible just for you:

Ezekiel 1: 4 "And I looked, and, behold, a whirlwind came out of the north, a great cloud, and a fire infolding itself, and a brightness was about it, and out of the midst thereof as the color of amber out of the midst of the fire."

That sounds way more like the description of an alien spacecraft than it does a visit from God. If you're not convinced to question the authenticity of the scriptures after all of these ideas, you should look up the "Vimanas". The "Vimanas" are flying chariots described in very similar detail to Ezekiel's depiction and found in Hindu religious texts.

According to the description in the Old Testament, angels are riding on their chariot that has four wheels (within wheels) and four cherubim, each with four faces. The chariot has orange light resonating all around it as it comes closer and closer. But that's only if you believe the story from the Old Testament. A little food for thought, the Book of Ezekiel is accepted by the Catholic Bible, the Hebrew Bible, and the King James Bible. It's funny to me that Ezekiel authored other writings that were not included in religious texts. That means it was decided that they could only believe part of his stories and not the other parts. I smell hypocrisy.

I am desperately trying to stick to the thesis of my book. But I suppose a few honorable mentions of unanswerable structures from around the globe couldn't hurt either. But it's only because of its relevancy to the science-fiction community and why they believe what they believe. With that being said:

The Ancient Pyramids—Not just in Egypt by the way. There are pyramids of incredible size, stature and architecture in Mexico, Egypt, India, China, and Peru. That brings up one of the most common questions: At a time thousands of years ago, when traveling across oceans in search of new lands didn't happen, all of these structures began going up and looking almost identical to one another. That deserves a little more credit than just being called an accident or coincidence. The pyramids in Egypt (there were more than just the three that were built in the fourth dynasty by the way) have baffled mathematicians, physicists, and engineers as far back as we can record. Part of the problem lie with the one thing that would answer everything . . . . evidence.

No one can seem to agree on the scientific data, not even scientists. If you know how serious and exact scientists and mathematicians are about their work, you can understand how frustrating it can be for them to not be able to find a solid answer. Historians lean toward suggesting the pyramids were built over a period of about a decade. The Great Pyramid of Giza, for example, was constructed with over two million blocks, each weighing an average of 1.5 tons. Some of the granite blocks on the interior of the Great Pyramid are estimated at 80 tons. If you follow the time span it means the Egyptians were able to accurately place three 1 ½ ton blocks, per hour, for the duration of the 10 year period. And all of this was accomplished with precision that leaves today's engineers scratching their heads.

I'm not a mathematician or a scientist, or anything for that matter; but that notion is difficult for my mind to comprehend. I know I have a small brain to most in comparison, but still, it's pretty tough to take. Most of the disagreement among when they were built and in what duration could be answered easily if the next obvious question could be answered: Where the Hell did they get the kind of technology to do it back then, if we can barely even do it today? How did a civilization with mostly stone and copper tools design and construct buildings that baffle today's scientists? Now add the depth and importance of that question to the first question of why we have pyramids all around the world, and you have a recipe for frustration and an incurable migraine. Now that I have you focused on that anomaly, we will move on to the next.

The Nazca Lines of Peru: Peru is a very popular place among ancient astronaut theorists. Apparently, aliens are hanging out in the most desolate, depressing places they can find. You know . . . . ancient astronaut theorists is a really long title. Can't I just call them nerds? No, no I shouldn't think like that.

Deep in the sun-drenched hills of the Peruvian desert, lay the Nazca Lines. The lines are no ordinary lines of any kind. They are actually described as geoglyphs. Geo for their geographical nature, and glyphs for . . . glyphs, the same meaning as every other glyph around the planet These glyphs are hundreds of feet, as opposed to a few inches. Most of them are either completely straight lines or they form pictures, that can only be seen from thousands of feet in the air. I warmly invite you to look it up for yourself as it is truly an amazing site.

The Nazca Lines however, in comparison, could easily be duplicated today. Although there is some ambiguity as to its exact age, most believe the Nazca Lines are estimated to be at least 2,000 years old. But in the case of the Nazca Lines, the question is not how they did it or how old it is? The question is why did they do it? Why would this primitive civilization build pictures that are only visible from the sky, at a time when the only creatures that should have been flying were birds? Is it perhaps because extra-terrestrials had visited Earth once, shared their technologies with humans, and the humans wanted to find a way to signal their godlike visitors from the sky to return?

Several nerds . . . I mean, ancient astronaut theorists, also postulate the idea that the symbols that still remain today are landmarks for the alien visitors to use as map coordinates. I'm sure a technology that can build spacecraft that fly at light speed, navigate through worm holes, and do all the other fantastic things that I unfortunately do not have the proper education to elaborate on, can find their way back to a point on Earth. I mean, we have GPS installed in almost every new car and we're nowhere near using flying saucers yet. But the people of that time would not have understood that and would have probably done whatever it took to get their beloved alien visitors back.

Wrapping up this much debated, geographical anomaly, I will make a few points for you to look into for yourself in reference to the Nazca Lines. Of all the images that remain today the three that always stuck out the most to me were a giant bird, a perfectly designed aircraft runway, and strangely enough, a picture of what appears to be a giant man. Is there a reason that the people of this desert valley created these certain images? Does the bird represent their interpretation of a UFO? Was the runway built by E.T.s or man, and was it used as an actual runway for the alien spacecraft? Is the oddly shaped, "giant" geoglyph their attempt to make contact with their distant sky-people? Stay tuned next week to be in just as much suspense because mankind probably won't have any answers by then either.

Moral of the story: Believing in aliens and U.F.O.s shouldn't make you an outcast because of what you believe. But it probably <u>WILL</u> make you an outcast for being a nerd.

CHAPTER 33

Atheists Beware

(No One Is Safe From My Satirical Kung Fu)

If you're an Atheist and you thought I wasn't going to pick on you just because I am an atheist, you are in for a rude awakening. Atheists are subject to just as much fault as anyone else of any other religion. They just don't believe in God. That's the only difference between the two. If you're an Atheist extremist you're just as dangerous as a Muslim extremist. Extremists are dangerous no matter which side of the coin you happen to be on.

I personally know Atheists that are so dedicated to trying to convert every Christian into an Atheist that they often forget that's one of the basic principles that they talk about. Their convictions are so strong that while talking about disliking it when religion is crammed down their throats, they end up cramming their non-religious views down other people's throats. Atheists are just as prone to hypocrisy as anyone else. If you hate it when someone does it to you, but it's different if you're doing it to them, you're being a hypocrite. Their preaching inherently turns them into the kind of people they were complaining about from the beginning. All I'm saying is, if you're going to talk about it, then be about it.

Atheists may not realize it, but the very same passion that drives them to preach about why there is no God comes from the exact same place inside of them and is the same passion that religious people claim they have for God. When they are preaching it is because they are filled with a deep, personal connection that makes them feel wonderful inside. Naturally, they want everyone else to share that same feeling. That's why so many passionate people look at you awkwardly when you don't get as excited as they are for whatever it is they are excited about. If you're not getting excited it's most likely because whatever they are passionate about may not be personal to you. That makes it practically impossible for you to feel the way they do.

I remember in 10th grade at my high school, one of my math teachers used to get so ecstatic when she would give her lectures. She could be explaining even the most simple of math formulas to us, but it didn't matter. Because to her math was her religion. I'm sure she also probably had some sort of faith but that's beside the point. She treated her lectures as though she were a Southern-Baptist minister preaching to her congregation. If she was even halfway through the class, you could bet there were exuberant hands-a-flyin' across that chalkboard, which matched the emotion pouring out of her voice. Back before the digital age, teachers used chalk and chalkboards to write out their work. Does anybody remember chalkboards? No? OK anyway, in her mind, math wasn't just a class that she taught. It was her life, and she wanted all of us to experience it the same way that she did.

Unfortunately, to much of her dismay, when she turned around to see the shared excitement on the students' faces, we didn't share one shred of enthusiasm about math. Could you blame us though? Come on, we were like 16 years old. Guys were thinking about sex, and the girls were thinking about . . . . What they could get out of guys for giving them sex. Let's be real for one second. 99% of the students in high school are not that on fire for math. In fact, math probably rates at the bottom of almost every student's List of *Things I Want to Do as Soon as I Get Home from School.*

There is a very common misconception that I would like to set straight. I was having a very in-depth, open-minded conversation with one of my peers in the Army about faith. My friend, who we will call Libidibi Mobdob for the purpose of irrelevance, enlightened me on this misconception; something I should have noticed way before but just never came to realize until he mentioned it.

"Libi" was a proud Christian, very trenchant and quite educated in several areas. His vast wealth of knowledge is one of the many reasons I respect him the way that I do. I was very glad when he agreed to let me use some of the discussions we had in this book. I had always enjoyed our debates in the past. He was a competition shooter and had traveled many times to compete with several different guns which I found to be an interesting hobby for someone that considered himself a man of

God. None the less, that sort of diversity in his personality confirmed my belief that just because you go to church and believe in God, does not necessarily mean you can't own a dozen guns and go shooting every month. Nor does it mean you have any intention of pursuing a career in the homicide industry.

Being a musician and my love for music gave us another common ground. Libi had also toured for a short time as a guitarist and a bass player. It was a nice change to actually be able to talk to someone that wasn't judgmental and offered insight and a vast opinion on some of my ideas.

Getting back to what I was saying. He knew I was an Atheist and was still able to carry on an educated conversation about faith. He said, "There is a difference between not having faith and being an Atheist."

A little confounded by the statement I replied, "I can't bring myself to place my beliefs in something that requires faith and no proof." I added, "And it is because of that that brings me to the conclusion that I don't have faith".

Libi argued that statement by saying, "Rather you realize it or not, you have a huge amount of faith, and just don't realize it."

"I have a huge amount of faith?" I said. I quickly tried to piece together the puzzle he had just placed in front of me. Basing my beliefs solely on the facts that:

(A) I didn't believe in Creationism and that life on Earth is a product of evolution
(B) I believed the Earth was billions of years old; and
(C) That I disagreed with the idea behind organized religion and following religious texts verbatim. It finally occurred to me that he was right.

Libi's statement brought about the simplest and yet somehow almost mind-blowing revelation. I place a lot of **faith** in the fact that I was not around to verify any of my beliefs any more than any true "believer". Further analysis revealed to me that my views or non-religious perspectives have nothing to do with a lack of faith.

In the end, Libi and I agreed that my faith was just pointed in a different direction, a direction that makes more sense to me personally, just like everyone that finds the religion they have been searching for.

A philosophical debate, yes. But a notable, fair argument. This scenario is just one example of how even though two people have different opinions on very serious issues, if you can stop and actually listen to one another, you can still learn something.

I hear a lot of people tell me that society would be unable to maintain civility if there were no fear of an eternal damnation of fire and brimstone or the repetitive experience of having your body being ripped apart over and over again. Levity is a very useful tool. I think one of the most common forms of levity is people sensing the presence of God, or the feeling of awesome power and acceptance that is uplifting. Literally hundreds of millions of people want that superb feeling to the point of intoxication. There are so many people that are unable to survive without that feeling once they have found it.

The misconception that most people fail to realize is that feeling is inside of everyone at all times, regardless of their faith in God. I can say that with veracity because I am an Atheist, and I'm still granted the pleasure of that same feeling. Everyone has the ability to receive that same feeling by other means. Singing is an uplifting experience. At least it is for those who can actually sing and don't sound like a male Silverback gorilla getting it on with a donkey.

There are a wide variety of illegal drugs that provide an equal or perhaps greater feeling than God can offer. I'm not trying to give legitimacy towards the use of drugs; they're illegal for a reason (most of them anyway). On that note, please do not go shoot up heroin or snort a couple lines of cocaine and claim you heard it was a good idea from me. I'm simply trying to illustrate the biological connection that our bodies feel from a stimulus.

There are other ways to equate the presence of God. Mathematicians, physicists, and other scientists get the very same feeling after figuring out a theorem or formula upon studying it for days, months, or even years. There is a phenomenally uplifting feeling that I truly believe stems from the realization of an epiphany. For me, the psychological presence is felt from many things. My passion for playing music, writing, and learning all lead to the same resonating feeling in the end, the presence.

There is one other factor that explains the relation of the psychological presence to the divine presence. Ironically, it's the easiest and most commonly overlooked one of all. It is love. Say what you want about me and my thoughts on life, but love can sum up in one word what couldn't be explained in 1,000. I love my two daughters so much that I get emotional and almost tear up when I hear them say, "I love you, daddy" or just think about hugging and kissing them goodnight. There is no question in my mind of how much I love my daughters. I would die for my two beautiful baby girls without the slightest hint of hesitation.

Now that I have explained the amount of love I have for my little girls, is anyone bold enough to claim that kind of love is different from the love people feel for God? Is there any father or mother that truly believes you can honestly say you don't feel the same way and wouldn't do the same thing for your children? I hope the answer is no.

Another belief of mine is that a lack of education is what separates the devout religious population from the Atheist and Agnostic community. And I don't mean a degree in the Old and New Testament or a PhD in being a good Christian. I'm not trying to pick on anyone particular with that comment. I only felt the need to add it because there are, after all, religious scholars and colleges strictly dedicated to the pursuit of an education based on Christianity. Learning years of information in any area would make you knowledgeable on the subject you studied. For that reason, I have respect for you if this happens to be your case. At least you know what you're talking about.

The only problem with that is after four, six, or even eight years of studying the Holy Bible, (or any religion) the only thing you are knowledgeable on is the Holy Bible. And if that is what you are passionate about at least you are being a real Christian and can honestly say you know what you're talking about. Education is the firm foundation of knowledge. Knowledge breeds understanding. Understanding leads to tolerance and civility, and I think civility is the key to the co-habitation of societies in our world.

I don't see anything wrong with wishing that the world was more educated, logical, and put their efforts toward something a little more useful to mankind. Seriously, think about all of the time, effort, and billions of dollars that are spent on religions worldwide throughout history. All of these people are spending one, maybe two nights a week at church when they could be educating themselves on physics, biology, astronomy, medicine, chemistry, or philosophy. Instead of spending years sitting in a church service that they don't believe in, bored out of their minds, they could be memorizing formulas to help cure cancer, AIDS, heart disease, Alzheimer's disease, anything . . . . Pick a plague.

As a last minute thought for this chapter, I would like to add a note to the other Atheists out in the world. You sons-of-bitches can be just as arrogant, hot-headed and pushy as any religious person out there. You guys act like you're better than everyone else. Every time I talk to someone that says they're either an Atheist or an Agnostic, it seems like they think they know it all and everyone else knows nothing. I mean, not me. I'm the exception. I'm an Atheist, but don't include me in that group. I really am better than everyone else, and I do know everything. Like I said, it's all of the other Atheists out there that are the problem, not me. Hopefully by this point, you realize from my sarcasm, I'm stating that I and every other Atheist out there are no better than anyone else in the world.

. . . Except Chuck Norris.

Moral of the story: No one deserves to walk with their nose in the air because no one is better than anyone else. Except for Chuck Norris.

CHAPTER 34

The Blind Leading the Stupid

The U.S. government is a shining example of a few elected officials governing the rest of the men and women of their country. That's called democracy. It's a relatively fair system of government. After all, there are far too many decisions that have to be made for the tens of millions of voters in the U.S. to take the time to vote on each decision that has to be made. The complexity and the countless number of bills that are continuously voted on by our government would baffle the minds of the everyday vital members of society.

Millions of people constantly complain that our government and its infrastructure have serious flaws. Yes, I agree that it does. However, this is the best that we have. I hate saying that, but it's the truth. Try seeing what life is like in countries like Iraq or Afghanistan for about a week, and I guarantee you will appreciate our country a little more. First of all, the system may have problems, but it's the individuals that become corrupt upon desiring power that negatively influence our government. Politicians are capable of being corrupted. Therefore, they have the power to corrupt the system and the laws that the government then approves or denies.

Even if we had a genuinely honest, hard-working person, that was driven to make the necessary changes for a better country, they are still vulnerable. Regardless of their intentions when they initially enter into politics, if they wish to be successful and reelected, they almost have to be corruptible. Think of it this way: You can have a high-tech, brand new school with 100 teachers, but if the teachers don't know anything or teach the students anything, the quality of the school doesn't matter. The school **SYSTEM** was fine, but the staff that ran it was not performing their jobs correctly. Here's an even better example:

You can go out and buy the best computer on the market, take it home, and hook it up. The moment a crippling computer virus corrupts the computer, from the inside, the computer may very well cease to ever function properly ever again.

Right about now, you might be asking yourself why I'm bringing politicians and governing bodies into this section. To answer that question, I enjoy explaining information beforehand so that people can actually understand the importance of the material. Otherwise, they will never really learn anything. It's that whole

"Give a man a fish and he can eat for one day. Teach a man to fish, and he can eat for a lifetime", or something like that.

The other reason is because I am about to discuss one of the most influential legislative bodies in history, one that I am sure many people are unaware of. That's a pretty frightening fact considering this legislative body's power has held strong for almost 1,700 years. I am talking about a meeting held under Emperor Constantine I, in the year 325 A.D. that became known as the First Council of Nicaea.

This piece of historical pie is overlooked by the majority of the Christian population. And it's a shame too, because after learning about it, it should do more than just entice you to raise an eyebrow. It should beg you to question the legitimacy of the New Testament itself. For anyone that just threw this book into the fireplace for saying something that contradicted what you think, thank you for being a true testimony to ignorant people everywhere that aren't willing to be open-minded and think for themselves.

So many people judge me over my opinion because, "You're trying to lead me astray from Jesus". No. No, I am not. I promise. Frankly, I don't give a shit what you believe, as long as what you believe doesn't harm anyone else. If you read this and find something you decide to research on your own, that you later discover you should have been inured about the whole time, you will have single-handedly made my day. I am not the problem. I am the messenger. And as the old expression goes, "Don't kill the messenger". That would suck. 'Cause . . . 'Cause I'd be dead. Yeah . . . With that in mind, let's discuss the First Council of Nicaea.

Matthew, Mark, Luke, and John all place emphasis in their books on the very last week of Jesus' life on Earth. The last supper, the Passion of Christ, and the resurrection are all mentioned in repetition by the apostles. It's interesting that the day that Jesus Christ was resurrected on changes every year. It changes because the Council of Nicaea decided to mark the day every year as the first Sunday following the full-moon after the vernal equinox (spring).

I should take the time to note that I understand the importance of celebrating the birth and resurrection of Jesus Christ, as it commemorates one's love for him. Some historians argue that December 25th was absolutely the birth of Christ because it followed a perfect sequence nine months after his alleged immaculate conception on the spring equinox, which at the time placed his birth nine months later on the winter equinox date of December 25th. There are other factors that you need to remember also. Depending on which calendar you are using the date of Jesus' birth changes. Some celebrate Christmas on January 6th or 7th.

With that in mind, there are many in the world that believe December 25th was not chosen because it was the closest calculated day of his birth. It was chosen to draw attention from the Pagan gods at the time, whose birthday was celebrated on December 25th. Believing in Pagan gods was considered heresy by the church. Placing Jesus' birthday on December 25th would allow the powers that be to gradually weed out the celebration of the Pagan gods as more and more men and women converted to Christianity in northern Europe. On a side note: The Jehovah's Witnesses do not celebrate Christmas or Easter because they believe it is wrong to celebrate Jesus' birthday and the day of his resurrection because they were determined by Pagan religions. Thus, it is disrespectful to Jesus. Score two points to the Jehovah's Witnesses for originality.

The dates of Jesus' birth and resurrection weren't the only things that were voted on at the council either. The council also wrote and placed into effect several new church laws, we call canons. These "canons" were rules of discipline that were to be practiced henceforth and were supposed to be unchangeable (that didn't happen). Some of them I find ridiculous and should have been obvious before they were made into church laws. But I was not around back then either. A few of these ridiculous canons were:

1. Prohibiting self-castration. (I don't know why this one needed to be made into law, as I think anyone could logically see why chopping off your own balls really sucks.)
2. Granting exceptional authority in regards to the patriarchs of Alexandria, Antioch, and Rome.
3. The prohibition of the removal of priests (Yeah, that's probably a good idea, right? Let's place someone in a seat of religious authority and make sure, no matter what, he will never lose his position). And I love this last one.
4. Prohibition of young women in the house of a male cleric because she may seduce and tempt him.

You know, after reading that last one, I'm thinking maybe they shouldn't have decided to do away with that whole, self-castration thing. I'm pretty sure it's in the very nature of humans to have physical and sexual urges. Mandating that you have to give up all forms of sex forever would almost make me want to cut my own balls off. And how exactly is cutting off my own balls supposed to bring me closer to God? I'm not implying that it's OK to be a rapist or a pervert. I'm just saying I don't see how anyone is going to be favored better in God's eyes by denying the very impulses that make us human. Correct me if I'm wrong, but I'm pretty sure the Bible even says that God created Eve for Adam to have a wife. Not that I give a damn what the Bible says, but you might. Civilization could not exist without procreation. And if God loves us all the same, stop suffering for no reason.

Christians aren't the first ones to offer sacrifice as a way to gain the favor of God. Religions have been performing sacrificial rites throughout history as a means to bring themselves closer to their deities. The Aztec, Inca, and Maya offered virgin sacrifices regularly by throwing them into a fiery pit or off a cliff in the hopes of their gods granting them with a fruitful harvest or healthy children being born. Those people didn't even see it as wasting human lives in the process. Boy, if the Muslims would have found out that those guys were killing their virgins, they would have lost their fucking minds, wouldn't they?

Even the legendary story of El Dorado (The Gilded Man or The Golden Man) tells of a village chief or priest going out on a raft, covered in a fine, golden powder, and throwing himself and hundreds of pounds of gold into the lake. The Meso-American people that are said to have come from this story believed that they would be granted riches in life, which is why they traded off the gold. Legend has it, the city was profoundly covered top-to-bottom with it; so it makes sense that they would trade the gold because they didn't need it. It wasn't what they valued. Speaking of the story of El Dorado, I actually wrote a poem about it because it's one of my favorites. I hope you like it.

The Golden Land

The road to riches beyond any dream
Drove many insane in search of the divine
The endless riches promised in the land
Would waste away lives and poison minds
What began in the middle of the lake
The golden man offered in prayers
Would all be lost to kings of greed
Where the scent of gold lie in the air
Through time and dredges the path was lost
Leaving only clues in the sand
The golden city was not made for lust
But to worship the golden land

Since we're on the subject of sacrificing things, let's talk about the idea of Lent. Lent has always been good for a laugh, at least to me. I'm not trying to be disrespectful; it's the truth. Lent has gotten out of control in today's world. People today are giving up everything from smoking, gambling, and sex, and even shopping, eating, and drinking. And it's all in an effort to demonstrate their love and devotion for God.

I find it ridiculous that we live in a world where hundreds of millions of people aren't willing to give up their vices just so they can be a better or healthier person. But we all have the ability to overcome adversity. We all have the ability to make the necessary healthy changes to our lifestyles. Why do people need to do it for God? Why can't they do it for themselves? They have the ability to. It's a fact. Someone once asked me what I was giving up for Lent. I told him I was giving up my New Year's resolution. When he asked what my New Year's resolution was, I told him it was to stop masturbating. Yeah, Lent came pretty early that year.

Now that my attention span has dragged me way off topic, let's finish by discussing the actual subject at hand. The other main argument that was hashed out, by the First Council of Nicaea, was the organized understanding on the divinity of Jesus Christ and his relation to God. It was decided that Jesus and God were one-and-the-same, even though one was a human and one wasn't. Jesus of Nazareth was henceforth **VOTED** into becoming the middle section of the holy trinity, the Father, the Son, and the Holy Ghost, by the men at the council. Disagree if you want to, but it's the truth.

Here's another fun fact that you might enjoy, or hate me for, one of the two. Emperor Constantine I only had the divinity of Jesus Christ answered because he wanted resolution on the subject. He was in charge over all of Europe and the constant questioning at the time was causing discontent among the people. You don't have to agree with me. It's OK. I won't even get mad if you quit reading right now . . . . I'll even wait for you . . . . Really? . . . . You're still reading? . . . . How lame is that?

Moral of the story: Get your facts straight before you bet your paycheck.

CHAPTER 35

Damn-It! Not another Rerun

History repeats itself. Everyone knows that it's true. Unfortunately, in the case of religion, the length of time between cycles is cut down dramatically, and just starts back to the beginning. 1200 years after the First Council of Nicaea, and one emperor named Charlemagne later, humanity found itself unable to stop waging war with other religions, as well as waging war within its own religion.

Yes, through Martin Luther's tireless efforts of disagreeing with the Catholic Church, and some of the more pedantic policies that they were introducing, the Protestant faith was born. From the 12th century A.D. and all the way through the 17th century the Catholic Church was seeking unachievable perfection through ideas such as indulgences, venerating Catholic saints and relics, and repeating the same prayer over and over again every painstaking week. The Catholic faith needed resolution and they found it (temporarily at least) with the Council of Trent.

From 1551-1553 theologians, scholars, and Catholic politicians . . . I mean bishops, all began hacking away at the predated, divine church mandate (again, written by man, by the way). After two years of writing all new edicts and reaffirming the old ones, in an effort to end the Reformation in Europe, nothing had been accomplished. In the end, the Catholic Church did not budge one inch toward creating a buffer zone between themselves and the Protestant faith.

Even though it was agreed that the Protestants would be heard while at the council, they were ultimately denied the right to vote on any of the issues. So as you can guess, they didn't bother to show up. I mean come on, who can blame them? That makes about as much sense as a dictator holding an election in which he is the only candidate running. And by the way, for anyone that doesn't follow history that

184

actually happens all the time in countries run by a dictatorship or totalitarian government.

One of the final edicts brought about by the Council of Trent was that the Catholic Church's interpretation of the Bible was nothing short of the absolute truth. Furthermore, any Christian who made their own interpretations of the scriptures was deemed a heretic. I guess I should be glad that I live in the world that I do. I may have a lot of things to complain about, but at least I can complain about them without being burned at the stake. For those of you who didn't close this book, curse at me, and begin writing me a long, nasty letter informing me of all of the reasons I'm wrong, I applaud you for having a good sense of humor during this exhausting reading. Who knows? Maybe somewhere out there in the world there is someone else who agrees with me that there was symbolic slavery throughout Europe long before there was ever slavery in the U.S.

By the way, lately I've been getting a lot of feedback from people telling me to not let any Catholics read my book out of fear of being martyred. If you're a Catholic and you happen to be reading this . . . wait . . . what am I saying? Let's be honest; if you were a true Catholic you probably wouldn't have gotten past page one. Lighten up people; it's a goddamn book. For anyone that is wondering, that concludes my thoughts on religion (for this book at least).

Moral of the story: It's OK to make a mistake as long as it's not the same mistake you made last week.

People Are Stupid

We must live in a society where it is perfectly accepted
If we choose to blindly hate
Where social class and political stance
Can force friends to separate
We must live in a society that values our image
And praises how we look
Where eating disorders overrule the need
To ever open a book
We must live in a society that values our color
And never values our worth
Where poverty can rob us of our acceptance
Even from the time of our birth
We must live in a society where religion can control
The way in which we live and breathe
Where mindless zombies cannot tell you the reason
Why they chose the religion they believe
We must live in a society that persecutes us
If we happen to be born gay
We live in this society, so please do not deny it
When I see it happen every day

CHAPTER 36

Men = Stupid and Women = Winy Bullshit

(There, I Finally Said It)

I don't know what's more difficult: discussing the controversial issues of religion or discussing the controversial issues of the male and female psyches. If there was any chance whatsoever that someone was not offended in the previous chapters of this book, I am sure this will take care of it.

Over the next few chapters (36-41) I will be discussing several of the problems that men and women are victims of in society, and man, is there a long list. The last few chapters of this book are more concerned with social conformity and why people feel the need to be like everyone else, when they don't have to. It's also about sex and lying. I don't really know what sex and lying have to do with the rest of this book, but hey, I've been told I make some good points. And you can bet there's going to be the same classic style of sarcastic, crude humor mixed into a strong rhetorical cocktail for the angry readers out there. Some of the issues I will be addressing in this section include:

1) Social pressure and conformity
2) Masturbation and the porn industry
3) Sex (the verb, not the noun)
4) The differences between the male and female psyche
5) Mixed communication among genders
6) Respecting each other reasonably in a relationship
7) Honesty

Hopefully, I'm able to still entertain while enlightening you through this last section of the book. I'm a little scared the first woman who reads this is going to email this whole section to every woman on the planet and absolutely destroy the possibility of me ever sleeping with another woman. Luckily, at this point, I've grown quite comfortable with masturbating. More importantly, I am a man of principle and stand by my lonely, tube sock convictions and ideals.

Conformity = You'll do it because it's what everyone else does and you need to fit in.

Let's start with answering the most basic question involved in social pressure and conformity, to get the ball rolling.

What is social pressure and conformity?

No problem. Let's dissect that to see if we can find our answer.

Social pressures are everything from peer pressure of alcohol and drug abuse, to having sex at a young age, and everything in between. The idea of social pressures obviously being society's idea of what is "In". Conformity is the members of society changing who they are in an attempt to make the team and be accepted as the "In" crowd. Therefore, social pressure of conformity = selling yourself out just so you can be considered accepted by the majority of society.

Not to sound like an after school special, but the truth is no one needs to sell themselves out if who they are in the first place is just fine. If who they are in the first place is a huge douche-bag, they might need to make some changes. But don't do it just to be accepted. Do it because you're a huge douche-bag.

I sometimes joke about Hollywood being the new form of cancer because it is slowly killing people in society. When I really stopped to think about it, it kind of is. Men and women, listen up. Stop trying to be Brad Pitt and Angelina Jolie. Not just because it's wrong to idolize someone strictly because they're famous, but also because it's really annoying to run up on what I thought was Brad Pitt and found out it was just a sad Brit.

Hollywood has its influence in everything we say and do. You see it everywhere you go. You wear it every time you get dressed. And you live it when you quote your favorite movie lines 50 times a day. Everyone, including myself is victim of it. Most of the time, it's like a bad case of indoctrination, one that has probably a larger influence than our parents and teachers combined when we were kids.

The idea that an individual's environment affects how they view certain traits can most definitely explain why some people in other countries prefer larger women, or hairy men, and other cultures have men that prefer trophy wives that don't possess a functioning brain, and women who prefer men that look like . . . . Matthew McConaughey.

The very same environmental influence can explain social thought patterns such as racism or religion. Other than the few special cases, if you grow up in a place where everyone in the geographical area is racist, and you are told that it's OK to hang black people because all black people are bad, you're probably going to think that it's OK to hang black people. If that's all you've ever known, that's all you've ever known. It also answers why entire towns and cities follow certain beliefs about ideas such as racism. If you've ever heard the expression "born and raised in this town" you understand exactly what I'm talking about.

I suppose, in the end, there are three factors, the psychological, sociological and external stimuli that are responsible for determining what one defines as attractive.

The psychological aspect involves personal life experiences that help mold who you are as a person. One example of this could be a man having a certain woman in his life while growing up, that he consistently interacted with and was of a certain separate image than what is commonly accepted as "hot". Even though society deemed her an absolute train wreck physically, he still found her attractive because she impacted his life in one positive way or another. The sociological aspect of which is the idea of whatever environment you grow up in will have an effect on the way that you think and your opinions and views. The final factor that affects how we view ideas, such as the definition of attractiveness, is external stimuli. The example of this that I like to give comes from a personal experience of mine.

From 2003-2004, while I was in Iraq the first time, I watched in only a few months, as the younger Iraqi women began going through changes in their physical appearance. Before you ask, no, I don't mean puberty. Iraqi women in their 20s and 30s quickly began attempting to look like the celebrities and models in American magazines. This quickly developed the idea that "this must be what every American woman looks like", which we all know is bullshit. In this example, the Iraqi women wanted to appear attractive to American men and changed their image, as well as their thoughts of what was sexy. In short, Hollywood was the external stimulus responsible for changing their perception.

America is no different either, and here's one of the most classic examples. Society watches TV and movies every day, and every day it's always the same thing: Muscular actors with six-pack abs and skinny, bulimic women with silicone boobs (which I'm not against by the way, but that's a different topic). Society sees this norm develop and begins to mimic the individuals because the people in Hollywood are treated with a higher prestige, presence, and appreciation. After all, nothing says beautiful, like vomit breath and the ability to play your own ribs like a xylophone, right?

It's in our very human nature to desire to be accepted, loved, admired, and appreciated. So I guess in essence, we all strive to be the bulimic idiots on TV and the big screen. That's the lesson we should take away from this example. Wait . . . That can't be right? What kind of a message am I sending? But if that's not true, then how else do you explain the recent change in young female Halloween costumes? In today's society, the sluttiest costume at the party wins. Men want to see drunk, slutty women on Saturday night, as naked as possible; doing things they will surely need to ask God's forgiveness for on Sunday morning.

It goes back to the most basic of men's needs and wants, which for a man are usually the same thing. Men and women are different on so many levels. Unfortunately for men, dissecting the female psyche can be comparable to trying to decipher the Rosetta stone, the real one I mean; not the computer-based language tool. I will also be explaining some of the most basic differences of the male vs. the female psyche. And I'm no Dr. Freud. I will be using realistic examples and not text book psychology so that even the most primitive of society's apes that call themselves men, can learn something from this.

Moral of the story: It's natural to want to fit in. But before you decide to change who you are, just so you will be accepted, ask yourself why you would want to be associated with someone that doesn't accept you for who you really are. Then have a bran muffin.

CHAPTER 37

Testosterone vs. Estrogen

(Male Psyche vs. Female Psyche)

Men are simple in our wants and our needs. We want women. We want sex. We want food. We want women to bring us food while we are having sex. We want to prove our manhood in ways such as hunting, fighting, killing, and finding ways to compete in all of those testosterone driven events. And then, we want to congregate with other men so that we can discuss, in primitive grunting usually, the sexual conquests, and triumphs in hunting, fighting, and killing we recently achieved. Yes, men are primitive.

Men want sex in the weirdest of ways too. We want sex in the morning, sex in the afternoon, sex in the evening, and sex right before bed. We want sex in the bathroom, sex in the bedroom, sex in the living room, and sex in the kitchen. Men want sex hanging from a ceiling fan, looking in a full-bodied mirror so they can give themselves a thumb's up admiring the curvaceous sexual conquest they believe they are satisfying. Men want irrational, gratuitous amounts of sex. Yes, men are primitive.

Women are slightly more complex. That was an unrealistic statement. Let me try that one again. If men are 4th graders learning their multiplication tables, then women are the complex mathematical formulas that explain quantum-fucking-physics. That's a little more accurate.

The average woman can have literally hundreds of thoughts in only a few seconds to a man's single thought over a few minutes. If the male psyche was hooked up and electronically monitored the thoughts of men, it would probably flat line. Women on the other hand, if hooked up, would most likely cause the machine to short circuit from attempting to process too many thoughts. It's true it's not always the case, but it is for this section of the book. Allow me illustrate my point.

<u>Female Thoughts</u>

"I need to do the laundry."

"I need to balance the checkbook."

"Did I forget to turn off the light in the bathroom before I left?"

"Why hasn't he called me back?"

"I can't believe they fired that new intern."

"I wonder how I'll do on my college finals."

"I hope he remembers I'm allergic to shellfish."

"What kind of car should I buy?"

"I have to pick up the kids from soccer practice."

"I need to make sure and grab dinner on the way home tonight."

"Where can I fit in time to go to the gym?"

"Does he still think I'm sexy?"

Male Thoughts

"Seeeeeeeeeeeeeeeeeeeeeeeeeeeeeeeeeeeeeeeeeeeeeeeeeeeeeeeeeeeeeeeeex"
"Foooooooooooooooooooooooooooooooooooooooooooooooooooood"
"More seeeeeeeeeeeeeeeeeeeeeeeeeeeeeeeeeeeeeeeeeeeeeeeeeeeeeeeeeex"

I'm summarizing the two genders to be humorous and illustrate my point, but it's still pretty accurate. Here are some other realistic examples separating the two sexes. Things like:

1) When women buy men a gift, it is planned out and purchased six months in advance so that it will be perfect and nothing will go wrong.

   When men buy women a gift, it is planned out and purchased six months in advance because they realize they are going to forget either her birthday or their anniversary, and it's just a good rule to always have a gift on hand.

2) When women want to buy a card for someone, they purchase the most thoughtful, compassionate, and sincere depiction of a spirit-lifting revelation.

   When men want to buy a card for someone, it is going to have something to do with sex . . . . every time. Seriously, the next time you're at a party for a guy, check out the cards. Chances are if it's from a man, it's got something humorous on it involving sex.

3) If a woman says she's not it the mood, it could mean 100 different things that men are expected to decipher.

   If a man says he's not in the mood, it means: If you move him the wrong way, he will most likely fart on you.

4) When a man tells his lady he's having an orgasm, it is happening at that very moment.

   When a woman tells her man she's having an orgasm, she is lying to him just so she can get the already annoying, painful sex over with quicker.

5) When a woman asks a man if the clothes she's wearing make her look fat, the answer is always "NO".

   When a man asks a woman if the clothes he's wearing make him look fat, he's gay.

6) Every man in the world knows that every woman wants to give him a blowjob.

   Every woman in the world knows that every man in the world is full of shit.

Moral of the story: Men are not from Mars, and women are not from Venus. Women are actually from Menstrual Hell, and men are actually from . . . . stupid, fat, "I can't believe she wants me to get off my ass and help with the kids" Hell.

CHAPTER 38

Wake Up! You Were Dreaming Again

I'm sure there are men out there right now who think that their women want to fulfill their every sexual fantasy without question. I'm also sure that I don't need to be a feminist to know that the majority of the women in the world will support me when I say, no they don't. That is a tragically misleading perception brought about by the very same overconfident male that thinks every stripper likes him.

This is your alarm clock people. Ladies, stop telling your man about things that he directly tells you he doesn't want to hear about. Guys, do me a favor and actually try listening and being a little receptive to your women. You might be surprised at the outrageously positive results from treating her as more than a-one-time-only hotel porn.

It's a matter of being realistic and considerate of the other person's position. Men, if you're still delusional enough to think you can figure women out, you might find your time better well spent learning underwater basket weaving. That probably has a better chance of being an applicable skill.

Girls, if you think your man is telling you the truth when he says you haven't gained a pound, when three years ago you looked like Kate Beckinsale and yesterday, someone mistook you for pregnant, I've got news for you . . . . He is lying. And he's doing it for you because deep down inside, it's what you want him to say. Men and women have got to stop sweating the small shit and start being realistic and honest. I didn't say hurtful; I said honest. But honesty is not being discussed so much right now because it luckily has its own chapter.

So, let's take a moment to look at some examples of men and women expecting some very unrealistic phrases to come from their better halves.

5 Things Men Should Never Expect To Hear From Women

1) "Oh, sure honey. I'll give you a blowjob while ironing your clothes, cooking your dinner, and cleaning the rest of the house."
2) "Honey, can we just do anal tonight?"
3) "I left you an ice cold case of beer in front of the TV so you wouldn't have to get up and see me taking care of the kids all by myself and be distracted from sitting on your ass the rest of the day."
4) "You know, it's been way too long since we've had a threesome with one of the women from the *Girls Gone Wild* videos."
5) "Guess what sweetie? I made your favorite for dinner tonight. We're having Megan Fox."

5 Things Women Should Never Expect To Hear From Men

1) "My queen, I left the un-maxable credit card in the new Prada purse that I bought you. Why don't you go take it shopping when you're getting your hair styled, a full-body massage, and a manicure and pedicure?"
2) "Hey baby! I just finished designing the invention you asked me about, the *Makes-you-orgasm-every-three-seconds Vibrating Recliner*."
3) "Sweetie, of course I want you to pursue your career in modeling while I stay at home with the kids."
4) "Oh my God! I woke up this morning with two sets of six-pack abs!"
5) "Megan Fox! . . . . GET THE HELL OUT OF MY HOUSE YOU UNAPPEALING ACTRESS WHO WILL NEVER BE AS HOT AS MY WIFE!!!!"

While we're on this particular topic, perhaps I should go ahead and include a poem that coincides with the same ideas.

<u>The Difference Between Us</u>

When will women realize that men cannot be taught?
If you think your man is different, I can assure you he is not
Men are simple creatures that never weigh the outcome or the cost
Men cannot stop for directions; they just drive around for hours lost
To a man there is no difference between a want and a need
They take pride in the number of women that have received their seed
When will men learn, women are impossible to understand
Don't feel bad men; it's not your fault, you were born a man
Women have complex emotions, usually more than one at a time
They want to be treated poorly, and they want to be wined and dined
They take pride that they control the frequency of sex
When a woman is hurt by one man, she takes it out on the next
A man's psyche will never change; it is how we are divided
If you try to change a man, you may find romance one-sided
Child birth <u>does</u> give women the right to be happy and then pissed
However, PMS is not an excuse that gives them the right to bitch
Not every man will lie and cheat; not every woman is a whore
Men and women are different from one another; that is all and nothing more

Now that we've established some ideas of what men and women should not expect each other to say, I'd like to close this chapter by briefly mentioning a few great marriage counseling tips that can be conducive for couples that bicker over the most meaningless bullshit ever imagined. Trust me, I've been there. Once a couple is officially "a couple", in a serious relationship, and no longer in the "oh yeah, we're dating, but I still bang other people" phase, a really good idea to implement is to sit down and create ground rules that are to be understood by both parties. Basic rules like:

1) No more banging other people on the side. This rule needs to be more than just understood. If a person is going to cheat on you once, they will be able to do it again. Not to mention the insane amount of trust issues that remain after it happens. Even if you decide to give the person another chance, there will always be a hint of doubt lingering. Chances are the person that was cheated on will constantly continue to worry and possibly bring up their lack of trust in their partner. I think you can figure out how many problems that can carry with it over time.

2) "I'm not your maid/butler." If a couple is living together, both members need to contribute to the daily chores and responsibilities, especially if it involves children, school, paying bills, cooking, and cleaning. If one person is sitting on their ass and the other is doing everything, it's a recipe for disaster. On the other hand, if ground rules are established, there isn't much room for questioning who the guilty person is. If a man, for example, establishes the understanding that his spouse, or girlfriend's, only responsibility is to be a trophy wife and look good on his arm, that's on him, as long as she keeps up her part of the agreement. If he starts to get too stressed out from his day to day plight, maybe he should have set up better ground rules from the beginning.

3) Space is good in a relationship. Again, this rule is even more important if the couple lives together. Too much time with the same person can get on anyone's nerves. It's also proven that time away from the same repetitive, daily stress factors can help revive one's energy and libido levels. Even something as small as scheduled girls night/guys night out regularly can help with this problem.

4) Last but not least, you need to establish a communication agreement. Regardless if it's two men, two women, or a man and a woman (because even gay couples still follow the whole "who's the butch and who's the bitch" in the relationship), if one of the individuals has my attention span, it might be a good idea to set up the understanding of, when it's time to talk, you need to give the other person your full attention. With me, it's mostly because I can't focus long enough to remember what my significant other is saying if the T.V. is on, or I'm playing World of Warcraft.

Those are just a few basic ground rules that can be applied to most relationships. And again, I'm just some idiot writing down thoughts and opinions about problems in society. I'm not even a real writer. I've probably failed more in my life than I have succeeded. I make $28,000 a year doing a job that I hate, and I still have the nerve to tell people to do what they actually enjoy for a living. Why the fuck would you ever listen to me? For God's sake, my extrapolation on the Eighth Commandment was a list of useless facts. What kind of shit is that? As a matter of fact, why are you still reading this? I told you back at the end of Chapter 34 to stop reading this. I'm full of crap! This whole book is a bunch of crap! . . . . Sorry about that. My evil alter ego got hold of the keyboard while I was thinking about the zombie apocalypse and decided to have a little fun.

Moral of the story: Don't let my alter ego touch my computer when I'm trying to write about information that I have no grounds to be educating people on. So, if you listen to me, that's on you.

CHAPTER 39

Sex: the First Place Every Man Goes

(and Every Woman Eventually Goes, but Still Pretends Men Are Sick for Going There First)

If you're expecting an elementary, science class version of coitus, you came to the wrong place. I would offer another disclaimer, but how many do I need to add before it's redundant? This chapter is going to be disgusting, depressing, funny, exciting, and interesting. So if you're prescribed a mood stabilizer and you haven't taken it, now might be a good time.

I am not going to actually define the word sex, but it's only because it has too many redundant meanings. Instead, here's a few of the words and phrases that are found to be synonymous with the word

<u>sex:</u>

The "Hustle and Flow"
Coitus
Intercourse
Relations
Flogging Molly
Porking
Boning
Giving the High, Hard One
Pressing the Flesh
Doing "The Do"
The Horizontal Mombo
Knocking Boots
Bumping Uglies

Going Heels to Jesus/Going 10 Toes to Heaven
Doing the "No Pants Dance"
Getting Tail
Making Babies
Putting a Deposit Down on Your Future Children
Knocking the Bottom out of It
And on a rare occasion . . . . Making Love

Oral Sex

Blow Job
Fellatio
All You Can Eat At the "Y"
Breakfast for Two
69
Eating Out
Tossing the Salad (Yes, it's still considered oral sex)
Traveling Down the Tunnel of Love
Deep Throating (for females . . . . and some of the guys out there)
Going Down and . . . .
Giving a "Rim Job"

We've already established that men are primitive creatures that think about sex more than Tom Cruise looks in the mirror to admire himself. And hey, I'm not saying I think Tom Cruise is gay but ummm . . . Yeah, I think Tom Cruise is pretty much gay. Look at the evidence. The Nicole Kidman break-up, the Katie Holmes breakup, the fact that he made out with Kelly McGillis, who looks like a horse that smacked it's face on a brick wall at full speed. And then there's the whole *Cocktail* movie. I'm not making reference to any one particular scene, just the fact that only a gay man could enjoy playing a role in that movie. Not that there's anything wrong with gay men. There's not. I love almost every movie with Ian McKellen in it. I think I deviated from my main idea again, sorry.

Anyway, this time we're going to get into just how disgusting men really are. I'm also going to elaborate on how often the average woman thinks about sex, and the false-innocent persona that most women would have men believe, and why it is all bullshit.

What Men Think About Sex

Men are disgusting. I'm sorry guys, but we are. It's the truth. Why else would we constantly be looking over our shoulders while we watch unnatural and unorthodox sex take place on the Internet? We're constantly looking over our shoulders because we know we're wrong and we don't want to get caught. You guys out there better not act like I'm the only one that's ever wandered off of generic porn sites when the pop-up blocker was failing to serve its purpose and let the curiosity truck run over the damn cat.

Men would watch porn all day and all night if we had no other responsibilities and wouldn't get caught. It's our nature. It's animalistic, and we're animals. Men would watch it and smack their junk around until they wouldn't even be able to get so much as a wiggle out of whatever name they happen to give their penis. Men would keep watching porn even after we couldn't do anything with our "Master of Ceremonies" so that the moment our penises can be abused again, we're ready. Men are disgusting.

All I have to say is, thank God the majority of the male population has to work to earn their living. It's called moderation guys. Get onboard. Without it, something as natural and human as masturbation can turn into a habitual problem that may very well take you down a path of sick, twisted shame that can only end with you praying to Patron Saint Isidore and attending some psychological evaluations to determine if you're a threat to society. In an effort to halt any of these disgusting atrocities from happening, I offer this advice: Just try to keep the numbers down to a realistic minimum, OK? It's not brain surgery.

When boys first discover masturbating, it's a lot like parents watching their son graduate from high school and go away to college. In either situation, your son is going to disappear all of a sudden, and you won't see him again for at least four years. When you're 13, masturbating is just part of your daily ritual. You don't give a shit. I know it was part of mine. That actually reminds me of a funny story.

I was lucky enough to never get caught masturbating by my parents. I wasn't, however, lucky enough to never get caught by my best friend. That is a very awkward conversation to have to sit through. I mean, I still finished. Oh yeah, the damage was already done. I might as well not let it ruin my fun; that's all I'm saying. If it's going to be awkward, it's going to be awkward. But awkwardness is just going to have to wait until after I'm finished. On a serious note, that is a very traumatic experience to go through as a child. And to this day, I still have nightmares reliving that terribly embarrassing moment, and I will wake up in tears. But then I perk back up because I realize I can use those tears for lube and go ahead and rub one out. For anyone who doesn't know that's what men like to call a "tear-jerker".

Men want doggy style all the time. Men want every sexual encounter to begin with oral sex and end with a "facial". Men want anal all the time. That is until they're privy to the nightmare-of-an-experience that can abruptly put an end to their ass cravings forever. Men want sex in the shower because it's clean. We want sex in the mud because it's dirty. We want sex on the beach, until we have sex on the beach and then we never want it ever again. That's one of those sexual experiences that are better left as a fantasy. Trust me, you will have sand in orifices that are very painful to try and clean out. And you know once you get it in there, trying to get it out is like trying to get an erection while staring at Bea Arthur in the nude; it's just not happening.

Now then, while you're trying to get that awful image of Bea Arthur out of your head relax and take a moment to read over a poem that describes the unrealistic sexual fantasy that men really dream about.

Every Man's Fantasy

It's strange to me I must admit
You were unlike any I've known in the past
You confided in me how much you love dick
And told me to spank your ass
I spoke poetry to you and you spoke of porn
At first I was lost and confused
You pointed to handcuffs and said to be warned
I didn't know I was about to be abused
I asked you about your life's ambitions
And you said, "Two girls and one guy"
I asked if you enjoyed music or fishing
"Not as much as giving head", you replied
You were not like the others that much was clear
You could strip to any song or beat
I had never met a girl who could look so sincere
While jacking me off with her feet
The truth is obvious, when you touch my cock
It's so clear that a blind man could see
I pant like a dog and get hard as a rock
Because you're every man's fantasy

What Women Think About Sex

OK ladies, sound the police sirens. You're busted. The days of getting men to believe that you are all innocent are long over. Do women think about sex with the same frequency and disturbing variations of rotary machinery as men do? No. Do they think about raunchy sex and want it way more often than they lead on? Yes.

The conflict with the majority of women is the balance of your body's natural sexual appetite and the morbid, male idea of "Every woman secretly wants to be a porn star". Then there's the fact that a few of the women in the world give the majority of women a reputation that is unrealistically attainable.

Some women do want to be porn stars. Perhaps not on the big screen, but definitely in the privacy of their own homes on amateur video cameras, usually with their boyfriends or their spouses endorsing the idea. When the camera turns on, for some reason, women turn into the sexual deviants that men have been masturbating to for the last 10,000 years.

For some women, sex is the passionate, thunderous depiction dreamed about over and over again and spawned from years of cheesy, unrealistic romance and sex novels. I'm only guessing here since I'm not a woman but I get the feeling that the women reading these books imagine themselves making love to a muscle rippling Spaniard who thrusts his huge member into the women reading the novel until she explodes at a climax as high as Mt. Everest . . . . Or some shit like that. I'm not a novelist. I write crude humor for adults that probably make up the bottom 15% of intelligence. I imagine if I had a crowd that found my writing entertaining it would be the sad, hopeless men of the world that still live in their parents' basement and beat off to a picture of Princess Leia in her two-piece from *The Return of the Jedi*.

To the women that fit the description of the lonely, sex novel reader, all I have to say is I'm sorry you never went to prom. Maybe you can go with one of the imaginary men from the novel you're probably reading right now instead of reading this. If you're pissed off, it means that it's true. So, my recommendation is to not get pissed off at me. Who's that knocking on my door at this hour? Oh, hey . . . . It's my old friend REALITY CHECK. Instead of getting pissed at me, try buying you some slutty outfits, thongs, and six-inch heels, and spend some time on the treadmill. Because guess what? That might actually land you the man of your dreams. More importantly, it will help you gravitate back to this planet and leave the previous world you lived in, in the embarrassing, sitting-at-home-during-the-prom past.

Moral of the story: Guys, take five minutes away from your habitual masturbation to breathe. Ladies, take five minutes from your cheesy sex novels to do the same thing.

CHAPTER 40

This Is Just for the Fellas

Fellas, it's time to listen up. I'm going to be letting you in on some information that you might want to know, especially if you're one of the millions of men that complain that their women don't want sex as much as they used to. What I'm about to say should be common sense. But let's face facts; men aren't always well-known for our strength in the common sense area.

First of all, women are not fucking light switches that can be turned on just by using your finger. Actually, that came out wrong. Obviously, that's one sure way to turn a woman on, but that's not what I meant when I said it. In the beginning of relationships, men and women are still in the whole fun, new, and exciting phase of the relationship.

However, after just a couple of years, that phase can begin to lose its spark. Sometimes it can begin to lose its spark after just a few months. In this particular case, things must be done in order to maintain the excitement and keep the sex life alive in the relationship. No matter what anybody says, sex is among the top three most important factors in a healthy relationship. Ask any marriage counselor and they will all tell you the same thing, I guarantee it. But you don't want to hear that from me. After all, I'm not a doctor, or a marriage counselor, or anything for that matter. What people do like to hear, for some reason, are statistics and facts. So, I did a little researching to see if my theories and ideas were correct. Here's some of the information that I found. To the men and women reading this, you'll be glad to know that having regular sex helps promote things like stress and blood pressure reduction and increased immunity. If you're trying to build intimacy in your relationship, you'll be glad to know that men and women experiencing orgasms together releases the hormone oxytocin, commonly referred to as the love hormone, which helps men and women build trust. In case you have never been in a real relationship before, trust is the key ingredient that helps increase intimacy.

Make no mistake my fellow horny males of the world, women want sex. If you happen to be a man worried about your lady losing her sex drive, here's a statistic to help shine a little light on your hormone-driven sexual worrying. Half of the women in America still want regular sex after four years of marriage.

But let me ask you a question (And by all means, since no one is around you while you're reading this, be honest with yourself). Would eating oatmeal for breakfast every day for years upon years get old? Yes, of course it would. Men don't require the same emotional and mental stimuli that women do to get us in the mood for sex. We're pretty much, just in the mood at all times that we're not sleeping. In the event that we're sleeping, we're usually dreaming about sex anyway.

Women on the other hand require certain aspects to be met just to place them anywhere near where men are automatically at any given time. Women cannot help the emotional and mental strains that they go through such as post-childbirth exhaustion from not sleeping, college on top of working full-time, abnormal weight gain, and even the natural loss of sexual appetite due primarily to the biological factors that accompany the aging process. These problems and several more I can assure you, are just a few of the reasons women's sex drive can go from a forest fire, to an iceberg.

Now then, it's time to move on to the men's contributing stress factors to women's loss in libido. Because men naturally want sex 150 billion times more than women (there's a strong statistic for you), we constantly want women to have sex with us at a rate that a bottle-nosed dolphin would be jealous of. Guys, if your lady gained weight and you forced her to either lose it or lose you; you're probably responsible for the loss of sexual appetite that follows. And it's not only because you made her feel self-conscious. Women that begin to starve themselves trying to lose weight too fast, often have a dramatic drop in libido, usually caused from the disruption of normal hormone levels from malnourishment. There are other factors that explain the female loss in libido, such as her partner's lack of physical attractiveness and biological fitness. In any of these cases, guys, try to be a little understanding and patient. I'm not saying to lie to your woman, just be understanding.

Now that your attention is on the obvious difference in male and female libido, let me pose another question to the men out there. More specifically, I am going to ask a question to the men who are fathers to young children, or at least have spent a lot of time around young children throughout their adult life.

When your children ask you for a candy bar when you're at the store and you tell them no, what do they usually do? They wait another 25 seconds and ask for a candy bar again. This time you tell them no in a more direct tone, reaffirming your already resounding "No" from before. So they wait another couple of minutes until you're at the cash register and ask for it again. Now you're frustrated, one of the kids starts to cry because they can't have it. All the while, the other kid is constantly grabbing things off the shelf that they shouldn't be, and you're trying to pay for your things while picking up the items that were knocked off the shelf. Now the children realize that they're about to leave the store without getting the candy bar that they wanted, so they make one last valiant attempt to persuade you by rolling their trembling, bottom lip and asking, "Please, can I have one".

At this point you just want to get out of the store because you're stressed out and you're holding up the rest of the line. So your answer is, "Oh, all right. Fine! Here, you can have a candy bar". Now, you had no intention of purchasing the candy bar initially when you first got to the store, refused several times, and finally gave in simply because you were tired of being badgered and just wanted to make them happy so that they will leave you alone about it. Now the next time you're out and you would regularly buy your kids a candy bar you say to yourself, "You know, they just got one the other day. They don't need one today". But of course, the kids don't want to hear that. So the cycle starts all the way over again and repeats until the parent is just going through the same pattern every time they're at the store. Hmmmmm?????

That sounds vaguely similar to a man asking his wife or girlfriend for sex when she was not in the mood in the first place. She initially refuses. He complains over and over again. She feels guilty about it. More realistically, she is probably tired after a long day of working, going to school, or taking care of the kids (and yes that is a full-time job by the way. I know because I did it), and she finally decides to give in and have sex. She doesn't enjoy it, so her desire for sex is gradually decreasing because it's becoming less and less fulfilling for her and becoming more strictly for the man.

The more this pattern repeats, the more the woman begins to think that her man doesn't even care about her point of view and that he is being a selfish asshole that doesn't appreciate her anymore. And I'm sorry guys, but she has a right to. Relationships only work when both parties are being considerate and understanding of the other person. It doesn't take long for women to completely lose their sex drive to the point of going through the repetitious motions that they've come to treat the same as taking their kids to the store and having to buy them a candy bar. Pretty soon, the other sexual problems begin to arise.

The man will soon realize that she doesn't want to have sex; so he in turn only asks for it when he gets sick of his masturbation and praying to St. Isidore because of his Internet porn addiction. But then of course, she doesn't enjoy it again, and the situation grows to be a self-feeding, relationship-ending problem that usually causes a lot more of the other serious problems that couples go through. It's a matter of being considerate of the other person. Guys, you've got to give your woman space, some time to breathe, and make her feel wanted. The more you make her feel like all you care about is her happiness, the more she will in turn, want to make you happy. And a big chunk of that is sexy lingerie, followed by a striptease and a blowjob.

For the men in the world that complain constantly that their women have lost their sex drive, I have two words for you: STOP BEGGING. The more that you ask for it when she's not in the mood, the more she will not want to have sex at all. I'm not trying to make any of the guys out there depressed. But come on guys. If you really want your lady to want you more and to get back to her XXX-Rated, fantasy-fulfilling, slutty, former-self, then you've got to do your part and give her a little initiative. After all, it's QUID PRO QUO. It's not QUID PRO . . . . SERVICE ME BITCH.

First of all, the chances of things getting back to the way that they were in high school and college are slim to none. That's the truth. I'm sorry if it hurts to hear it, but I'm a firm believer that if it hurts to hear it, it's probably true. There are several obvious reasons for this that I shouldn't have to name, but in an effort to take up more white space, what the hell, you know? For example, one of the first things to happen (and it happens all too often, by the way) is women getting pregnant and beginning to have children too early in their lives. There are so many cases of women that get pregnant at a point at which they haven't even finished college, started their career, and in some cases, even finished high school. That can put a serious damper on a woman's sex drive by the time she's in her mid-to-late 20s. That's a depressing thought for both genders considering, on average, women's sexual prime is during their 30s.

By the time they're 25 or 30, they already begin feeling regret, not for having their children, but just for doing it at such a young age because they've lost so much of the freedom they had before. Rather the men out there want to accept it, women want to be care free, fun, and do the things that they used to. Unfortunately, many of them have real world shit to deal with that takes up most of their time and energy.

Women want and need to feel sexy and desired. It's a fact of life, especially when referring to something as personal as sex. And if she thinks you're only having sex with her just so you can get off and you don't care about her happiness anymore, how is she supposed to get turned on by that? Try placing your lady's feelings first and not just for a day so that she'll think you're being sweet, just so she can then find out you only did it so that you could get yours again either.

You're actually going to have to put forth an effort my friends. Try going weeks without sex (you're probably already doing that anyway). And you should not only not ask for sex, you should try denying her after she comes on to you the first time. Don't be a dick and make her feel disgusting and turn her away; just try a little bit of playful banter and build the suspense in your sex life back up. Every man and woman want what they can't have. It's a story as old as time. Man wants a toy. Man gets the toy. Man plays with toy. Man quickly begins to lose interest in the toy because he was able to get it. That's why it's so important for women to hold off on having sex if it's going to be with someone you actually care about. If it's casual sex, who the fuck cares? But if it is with someone you genuinely want to be with, and the man is able to get the "toy" on the first day, he's going to lose interest shortly after. Women are no different. The same anticipation that works on men, works quite well on women too. However, with women, the sexual anxiety is more about getting what she wants. When women are rejected, it becomes a playful game that they take upon themselves to win. It's a really fun game if you've never played it, by the way.

A man needs to make a woman feel appreciated and let her know that you think of her as more than just a collection of used orifices. I guarantee that if you're being considerate of her feelings, the return on your thoughtful investment in your relationship will more than likely come back to you in the form of a fun-filled evening that leaves you sleeping the entire night with a smile on both of your faces. I mean, let's be honest here. That's what it's all about, the excitement in the bedroom. The kids, the money-handling, and the sharing of hobbies, you can do all of that with a roommate. Very rarely will a guy ask his male roommate to dress up like a naughty school girl and do a striptease for him. I'm sure it happens, but I still think it's pretty rare.

Remember back in high school and college? That whole cat and mouse game that made the relationship game fun. That's what you need to get back to. Way back when, when you were never sure if you were even going to get laid. That's one of the reasons the sex was so great. It had spontaneity.

One of the saddest things that I've ever heard one of my friends say was, "Yeah, I'm planning on having sex with the old lady this weekend". I remember thinking to myself, "Wow bro; I can't imagine why your wife gets drunk and tells us your guys' sex life has gone from fervent and alive, to a dead fish that washed ashore. You know the kind, right? That fish that's on the beach that everyone sees, but everyone acts like they don't see. They just think, "Ewww, that's gross. Somebody should get rid of that, but I'm not gonna be the one to touch it". And that's probably what your wife thinks about your penis . . . . It's a dead fish that she doesn't want to touch.

Moral of the story: Less is more. The less you ask for it; the more she will want it. Just make sure you give it to her when she asks for it. Unless you want your penis to be thought of as a dead fish, remember that relationships are reciprocal.

CHAPTER 41

"I Only Said I Loved You
So That I Could Get Laid"

("Oh . . . . Well, Why Didn't You Just Say So?")

Finally, I get to talk about what I think is the most important issue in relationships. And that important issue is called honesty. Honesty is the very backbone of relationships, marriage included. It's true, I may not personally believe in the institution of marriage in today's society because of how much it has changed; but that doesn't change the fact that if you are going to have a successful marriage, you're going to have to have honesty. Remember, I said HONESTY. I never said cruelty. There is always a kind and fair way to be honest, especially if the issue you are being honest about is difficult to discuss.

So much drama encompasses relationships that it's no wonder people lie to one another the way they do. They're trying to avoid any unnecessary drama that may be brought about from whatever they're being honest about. The trouble with that scenario is that the longer you put something off out of kindness (and by kindness, I mean lying), the more painful it is going to be when the truth is finally revealed. What's worse is that if you're not honest then you're adding to the problem at hand, no matter what the situation is. It doesn't matter how you try to rationalize it, it's never a good idea. I promise. It might seem less painful or less stressful by not telling the truth because you don't want to hurt the other person's feelings, but in the long run, you're going to save both of you a lot of time and stress that can be avoided by being honest right now.

To help illustrate my point, allow me to throw an example at you. And by all means, if you disagree with my ideas, it's OK; remember,

I'm not a psychologist. I'm still going to think I'm right though. That's confidence by the way, not arrogance. I know that because I am confident that I'm not going to care if you agree with me.

(SITUATION) Bob and Lisa

Bob and Lisa have been seeing each other for approximately two months. Lisa decides that she doesn't want to date anyone else and has felt that way for the past few weeks. Bob also has no desire to see anyone else. However, he is just not ready to get back into a committed relationship because of past experiences. Then comes the awkward moment of honesty vs. saving Lisa's feelings.

Lisa asks him if he would be OK with taking the next step of being in an official committed relationship. She also does the right thing by telling him it's OK if he doesn't want to; but if that's the case, then she thinks they should go ahead and split up because she feels she's getting too attached and if he's not ready, it isn't fair to either of them. Way to go Lisa! You did the right thing (For the moment that is).

Now comes the first mistake. Bob really likes Lisa a lot. She's beautiful, fun, down-to-earth, and best of all, she loves giving him oral sex. So, while she is telling him how she feels and what she wants, Bob thinks to himself, "Man, Lisa is a really cool chick, and I really like getting head. Maybe I can just lie for a little while and hope that I do get to the point that she's at right now?" Wrong answer, Bob!!!! Bob, you just lied to your lady for no reason. What you should have said was something like, "I understand. We've been together for a couple months now and you're right, it's not fair to either of us if we stay together and we don't feel the same way for each other". Or perhaps even, "Well, that makes a lot of sense. I guess we should go our different ways. If nothing else, I hope we can still be friends".

But no, Bob, you dumbass, you had to go and lie to her. So just for fun, let's fast forward a couple more months into the future shall we? Now the not-really-happy couple has tension and awkwardness between each other that neither of them is willing to talk about. Lisa doesn't want to say anything, because she has developed such strong feelings for Bob that she doesn't want to lose him regardless of the awkwardness between them. Bob doesn't want to say anything because that would mean he would have to admit (that means being honest) that he lied to her, and he also doesn't want to hurt her feelings. Oh and then there's the whole oral sex thing too.

The two are now faced with the next dilemma when Bob does the right thing and asks her if she feels an obvious, awkward tension between the two of them. Good job, Bob! Way to learn from your mistakes. Unfortunately, it's Lisa's turn to be stupid and lie rather than face the truth. She tells him no, of course. He reluctantly feels even more awkward because now she knows that he obviously feels awkward, but she says she doesn't. So now he's in an even more difficult spot than before. Lisa, you dumb bitch. You should have just told him the truth. It wouldn't even have to be anything elaborate, just honest. A simple, "Kind of, yeah. Why? Do you feel awkward around me?" would have sufficed.

Never has there been a more ridiculous, useless idea than lying. Don't get the wrong idea by me saying that. I don't want anyone to think that I've never lied, because that in itself would be a lie. The difference is how much we choose to lie and what we choose to lie about. That being said, I definitely tell the truth a lot more than most people that I know. Anyone that knows me can say without a shadow of a doubt that the term "brutally honest" is completely justified when speaking on my behalf. I guess I just don't think that people should get mad if they ask you a question and you tell them the truth. Again, you can be respectful while being honest. That's why I tell everyone, "Don't ask me questions to something that you don't want to hear the answer to". It's like the perfect, little public disclaimer that completely puts the blame in their hands.

Moral of the story: Which one sounds better to you? Lying to avoid confrontation and ending up with ten times the confrontation because you let it balloon; or calmly and rationally offering the truth in a respectful manner that doesn't leave room for questioning or doubt?

CHAPTER 42

Defying the Laws of Physics

Lying isn't just hurtful in romantic relationships either. Lying is hurtful and pointless, period. I'll explain what I mean. Lying is one of the most common mistakes made by the members of society. It's stupid and pointless and it doesn't resolve anything. Sometimes though, there are those that go beyond the ordinary bounds of ridiculousness. I can't talk about people refusing to tell the truth and not poke fun at pathological lying, or as it appropriately termed by psychiatrists "pseudologia fantastica". You should know it by now. Just like a fat guy staring down a cupcake. We all know what's going to happen next. So with that in mind, prepare to be educated on society's own little real-life punch lines.

Pathological liars lie even when it's usually easier to just tell the truth.

They love to get really descriptive in their lies too. It's hilarious. In fact, sometimes I think some of the people that I've known who were pathological liars could have made excellent fictional authors. The next time you're around a "patho" stop and ask them how their day was. As soon as you ask, you're probably safe to pop some popcorn, sit back, and enjoy the fictional roller coaster that they will almost certainly take you on.

Pathological liars used to make me mad when I would listen to them. Luckily for me, I can now just laugh at them and shake my head with a sense of sorrow and pity. What's funny about pathological liars is that their lies aren't bound by any sort of reality. The best stories are when they try to bring someone else into their unbelievable story that completely cuts them off by saying, "Whoa! If you want to make up crazy shit, that's fine. Just don't drag me into that distorted, fantasy-world that you live in". The other one that I love to laugh at is when they're telling a story/lie that they forgot they told you before and completely change the story/lie from the original. On the other hand, it's great when you're bored and looking to be entertained.

What's even weirder is when the story they decide to chime in with has nothing to do with what you were talking about. You know, like you're just having a regular conversation when the person drops in with, "That's awesome guys. Did I tell I just got 24 karat gold rims put on my truck?" You're standing there confused like, "Dude, we were talking about how to properly cook squirrel before you eat it. What the fuck, bro?" (Never mind the fact that I could see his truck from where I was standing at the time and . . . . No . . . No he didn't).

Another weird trait among pathological liars is that it doesn't matter what you're talking about, they feel the need to chime in with a story that allows them to exemplify themselves among the rest of you. That's a really fancy way of describing the person who always feels the need to "One-Up" you. And that shit gets old quick. If you tried telling a simple story that ends with a funny anecdote about you locking your keys in your car, the "patho" sitting next to you would interrupt you with something like this:

"No shit, there I was, by myself. The volcano behind me that had just erupted was sending lava straight my way. My keys were locked in the car and if I didn't get them out so that I could escape, the volcano was going to claim me as one of its victims. Suddenly, I remembered a piece of the training that I experienced that the government wasn't able to erase when I gave up my previous career as an international super-spy. I pulled out my hair comb which was also flamethrower and cut through the door locks and opened the door. With no time to spare, I used my ninja-like reflexes to grab the keys, put 'em in the ignition, and drive away like I did in one of my other former careers as a professional race car driver. Yep, that's what happened."

Yes, anyone that knows a true habitual liar knows that story is not beyond the boundaries of their reality. The other common theme among "pathos" is that they love to use other people's stories. This one is especially funny if the story that they stole happens to belong to the person they are telling the story to. You want to talk about an awkward moment? That one takes the cake.

You don't even have to be talking to them. Trust me. I know it for a fact. There is a really awkward moment when two friends are having a funny discussion about how penguins get to wear a tuxedo year round, and their other friend/liar interrupts as soon as he can get a word in by saying, "Yeah, that's hilarious. You know, I've been to Antarctica? It's actually not that cold there, surprisingly".

I'm not confirming that particular story actually took place. But if it did (when I was 27 by the way), the average temperature in Antarctica is between—112 to—130 degrees Fahrenheit throughout most of the year.

Usually it's pointless to try and confront a pathological liar about their lies because they simply lie deeper and deeper to get out of the first lie.

The truth about what causes pathological lying is actually pretty sad. It usually originates from years of attention deprivation from family and friends. This leads to a lack of self-confidence and can eventually matriculate into severe social-awkwardness. In an attempt to get back the starved attention, affection, and social-structuring of their childhood years, these lonely individuals begin to make shit up to make themselves sound more interesting. It's logical when you think about it. They want people to like who they are so that they will be given more attention.

In most cases of pathological lying the individual began telling stories in their youth that just slightly stretched the truth in order to make the story sound better. After years of smaller lies, the stories become more detailed and less bound by the laws of physics. I only make that exaggeration because if you've known as many of them as I have; you would swear some of them thought they were Neo from "The Matrix" with how much ass they thought they kicked. Getting back to what I was saying though; eventually, in advanced stages, the stories that are completely fictional can begin to feel like actual memories to the person. So much so, in fact, that many of them believe they are telling the truth and don't even know when they lie anymore because their stories have truly become their reality. And as much fun as it is for me to poke at, it's still sad.

Ever have a friend or a family member who is a pathological liar? That's even worse than talking to someone you don't even know who's a "patho". That can be embarrassing around your other friends that don't know it. Especially if the person is far enough along that they have become one of the people that live in "*The Matrix*". That's not fun.

That's humiliating. By any other standard, we would call that person crazy. But no, we just let them go on living their continuous web of lies. Watching a patho tell a story is a lot like watching an episode of *Scooby Doo*. You know for a fact that dogs can't talk. But it doesn't stop you from laughing hysterically at the ridiculous display of fiction that's in front of you. There. I said my piece on that subject. Now I can let it go.

Moral of the story: You don't need to make up outrageous stories to get people to like you more. You just have to buy them beer and pizza. Who wouldn't appreciate that? Seriously though, ignore what I just said. In truth, you only have to buy Alex P. Hewing beer and pizza.

CHAPTER 43

World of Warcraft

(1/2 Video Game, 1/2 Meth)

This book could probably survive just fine without me including this chapter on addictions in its composition. But I would be remiss to not include one more classic example of people being dumb. Raise your hand if you have ever heard someone say, "The first one's free". According to a recent fictional study that I'm making up at this very moment, statistics show that there is a 147% chance that whatever you are trying for the first time is going to get you addicted to it. That holds true for any addiction, and not just drug addictions.

About three years ago I was addicted to World of Warcraft in the worst way. The previous three (or so) years prior to that I had spent ridiculing anyone that played games like World of Warcraft. I broke down after a friend of mine asked me, "Have you ever played it". It occurred to me that I really had no right to make fun of anyone that plays games of this nature, because I had never tried it for myself. He told me, "You have nothing to lose. You can even download the game and try it for free all the way up to level 20". So I figured, what the Hell. At least if I didn't like the game I could then feel better about making fun of my friend again. I had no idea what events would unravel from a simple choice to play a game only one time.

World of Warcraft is by far the most addicting video game that I have ever played in my life. I'm glad that I'm free of it now. But my God, that shit was good while it lasted. I actually reached a point of using the terms "Crack" or "Meth" when referencing the game to other people while I was addicted to it. The reason Blizzard allows us to download the game for free initially and build your character all the way up to level 20 is simple. That shit is exactly like crack or meth.

You will not be able to put it down, and you will keep coming back for more and more. For me, World of Warcraft was a lot like my penis after I discovered the joy of masturbation. I could look you in the eyes and tell you I was never going to touch it again, but it wouldn't matter. You would always know that I was lying. I've taken the liberty of creating a fun list to illustrate other similarities between games like World of Warcraft and meth-amphetamines. Things such as:

- Both addictions cause someone to lose a considerable amount of sleep, causing the appearance of what I call "the zombie gamer".
- Extreme cases of gaming addiction can lead individuals to malnutrition by completely forgetting to eat or skipping meals because of the duration of time that it would take to make the food and eat it.
- Drugs end relationships and marriages. Well guess what? So do video games. If you don't believe that check out this little fact: At a Blizzard Convention, men and women were interviewed that had recently divorced their ex-spouses because they "got in the way" of spending more time on World of Warcraft.
- Drugs can cause people to lose their jobs, and once again, so can video games. There are people that leave work, go straight home, immediately got online, and stayed on it until it was time to go to work the next day. Unfortunately, because 16 hours passes since the last time they were at work, and they hadn't slept in over 24 hours, they're constantly calling out of work so that they catch up on sleep and not come into work with a "zombie gamer" appearance. You can guess what ultimately happens.
- Drug and video game addictions frequently force lifelong friends and family to become estranged. I can't even count how many times I canceled plans with my friends and family and was forced to hear, "Goddamn it! It's that fucking game isn't it? I knew it! You just can't put it down, can you? You need help bro." And I did. I did need help.

Luckily, today I am much more poised than I was back then. I now understand the value and importance of the word moderation, thanks much to my ex-wife Angel and my friend Doc Workman. Doc showed me that there is nothing wrong with enjoying a hobby as long as the hobby doesn't get in the way of everything else or damage my relationship with my friends, family, and my responsibilities such as work, school, and proper parenting. Angel showed me that . . . . You know what? Angel showed me that if I didn't stop playing the game long enough to pay attention to my duties as a father and a husband, I would have divorce papers waiting for me. And she was completely in the right for being so stern with me. I deserved it, and it was what I needed to hear. I'm just glad that I wasn't one of the people that decided to get divorced because my spouse was "getting in the way of my World of Warcraft playing". Granted, we ultimately ended up divorced, but it was after I had quit playing and was more because we just grew into different people.

WoW isn't completely to blame either, by the way. All Blizzard did was create a product that people would keep coming back for. The responsibility of moderation is left to the people playing the game. You don't blame McDonald's when a fat guy dies from eating too many Big Macs. You blame the dumb fatass that can't stop himself from eating his problems away. The same can be said for World of Warcraft or any other video game. It's not Blizzard's fault I wasn't man enough to handle playing the game a little each week and still remain responsible enough to remember my duties to myself and my family. I may have become way too enveloped into World of Warcraft. But believe me, that shit is really good.

It may be very easy to make fun of someone like me, who becomes addicted to a video game that I used to make fun of other people for. But the truth is addictions are no laughing matter. The constant feuding among addicts and their loved ones is difficult to describe, let alone endure. The helpless feeling of watching someone that can't stop repeating the action that's causing their loved ones so much pain is disheartening.

If you're the one trying to help an addict through their time of need, my heart goes out to you, especially if the person is a drug addict. Drug addiction is much worse, in all seriousness, because drug addicts will sell their belongings to get the money they need to buy more drugs. They will lie to anyone if it means getting one more small taste of whatever toxic chemical they are poisoning their body with. Parents will steal from their children. Children will steal from their parents. Felonious crimes such as murder, theft, and extortion become everyday actions to innocent men and women that would have never considered committing crimes such as these before they were addicted.

Moral of the story: Crystal Meth will land you in the hospital. Your friends and family are the ones that take care of you when you get out. Make sure you choose the correct ones that you want by your side.

CHAPTER 44

I Can't Figure Out Why I'm So Fat? . . .

(America Seems to Say)

The previous chapter centered on addiction, one of the most common forms of stupidity among society, and I thought it only fitting to make the chapter that sequentially follows it another common demonstration of how stupid people can make poor choices in health and fitness. People can recognize that it's wrong to poison our bodies with heroin or crystal meth, but we're apparently fine with cramming our bodies full of crappy food or living unfit, unhealthy lifestyles that will ultimately kill us. Personally, I don't see the difference.

I love to give people famous quotes almost as much as female porn stars love to give head. Another one of my favorite quotes of all time comes from Albert Einstein:

"The definition of insanity is doing the same thing every day and expecting a different result."

By Albert Einstein's definition (which I completely agree with), I think the majority of Americans are insane. Let me explain why: How many people eat junk food every day, get fat, and say, "I can't figure out why I'm so fat?" If you're asking that and you're being honest, you're a moron. This is a classic case of people not doing basic math and actually allowing the problem to happen. First of all, there's a big difference between having a few extra pounds on you, and being the definition for the medical term "morbidly obese".

I have a few extra pounds on me; I think it's like eight lbs. that I need to lose to be at the perfect "ideal" weight for my height. The real risk comes into play with people that are actually fat. I'm talking about guys with a severe case of "forgetting what my dick looks like".

If you want technical, medical lingo, fine. How's this?

Obesity is an excess of body fat has accumulated to the extent that it may have an adverse effect on your health, leading to reduced life expectancy. Obesity is equated to a body mass index (BMI) that is greater than 30 kilograms (approximately 14 lbs.) per square meter. In America (because we're the only ones that aren't onboard with the Metric system) the equation is BMI = lbs. x 703 / square inches. So, basically what I said earlier, right. And let's be realistic for a second. 14 lbs. overweight isn't that big of a deal. I'm talking about dangerous levels of weight gain. People that are 50 or more lbs. overweight need to start making some serious lifestyle changes. I'm not trying to be a dick. I'm just being real. While 50 lbs. overweight is definitely not a huge health risk in comparison to the people that are 100-200 lbs. overweight, it's still a serious situation. And here's why.

50 lbs. can quickly turn into 100 or 200 thanks to another problem that almost always follows obesity known as laziness. People begin to lose their confidence and assurance of their self-image. This can cause feelings of doubt and questioning the value of someone's own self-worth. The next ugly step to follow is the inevitable "I don't know why I should even bother trying to lose weight now. It's too late. I hate myself". In the end, they give up attempting to live any sort of a healthy lifestyle and begin to gain weight even faster. Pretty soon the health problems begin to show their ugly faces, with things like diabetes, heart disease, and osteoarthritis. If anybody out there thinks that's not a serious problem, you should consider the fact that severe obesity (BMI > 40) reduces life expectancy by 10 years on average, and in the United States alone, obesity cause approximately 110,000—350,000 deaths every year (depending on which health magazine you're reading).

You don't even have to lose weight for the obvious reasons of having a better self-image or more confidence and libido. You should do it for your family's sake. Try putting your children, parents, and brothers and sisters feelings first. I doubt they want you to die before you absolutely have to. Furthermore, allowing yourself to reach that state of poor health simply because you're lazy is very sad and pathetic. If you don't want to consider your family's happiness, maybe you can consider their misery. How much do you think they will enjoy having to take care of you because you let yourself become so physically weak that you can no longer wipe your own ass?

You can do it for your own happiness if nothing else. Do it because you want to be able to play with your children without needing to stop and grab a puff from your inhaler, a shot of insulin, and a nice half-sheet of cake to get the energy to not fall over and pass out. Do it because you want to be able to dance at your daughter's wedding or walk her down the aisle without going into cardiac arrest.

Do it so that you can get your sex drive back because you look and feel sexy again. Guys, do it so that you can finally find your penis again. Ladies, do it so that guy at the coffee shop won't be able to stop undressing you with his eyes while he stares you down and smiles at you. Frankly, I don't care why you do it. Just please get it done. And do it soon because with the rate that fast-food restaurants are popping up, it's going to be really fucking hard to find a place that serves something other than a heart attack and a side of diabetes.

Now that I got the unhealthy food portion out of the way we can discuss the other important factor in the equation, exercise. Exercise is great for burning off some of the calories that you took in that day. It helps build and tone muscles, strengthens the heart, and best of all, helps relieve some of the guilt of being overweight and eating too much crappy food. But of course, we can't have a healthy choice like exercise without having the X factor known as moderation. The rules are the same across the board. Exercise and fitness is extremely addicting for a lot of people. Some people can't handle a little bit of fitness. They need to start off with a 12 mile run, follow it up with a two-hour weight lifting session, two protein shakes, and a double-shot of steroids. That's a formula for small testicles and a huge ego if I ever saw one.

The guys that are addicted to lifting and exercising want muscles on top of their muscles. They want cut lines on top of their cut lines. They want to be so big; they have to buy a tool to help them wipe their ass because they can no longer reach far enough back to do it themselves. Yes, moderation truly can be applied to so many things. Just try to remember: Too much of anything can lead to small testicles.

Now that I've roasted the muscle bound dick-headed males out there, it's time for me to wreak havoc on the 85 lb. women out there that think they need to stop eating as soon as they finish a crouton and immediately go run a marathon. Anorexia nervosa and bulimia nervosa are probably the two most common eating disorders among the supermodel wannabes of society. I'm sure we're all familiar with them both but just in case: Anorexia is starving yourself to the point of malnourishment because of constant fear of weight gain and an irrational perception of your own self-image. Bulimia is the binging followed by the immediate purging of the ingested food in an effort to negate any calorie intake and weight gain. Of course, bulimia also carries with it several of its own health risks just like anorexia. Some of bulimia's more notorious health problems are dehydration, chronic gastric reflux, infertility, and Boerhaave Syndrome (the rupture in the walls of the esophagus). Bulimia is considered by most health professionals as less life-threatening than anorexia, but it is far more common.

It's also completely disgusting. I don't know what the Hell these women are thinking. I mean, yeah it's true all of that constant vomiting can give you a skinny figure. But what good is a girl that looks like that if I can't go near her because her breath reeks of vomit. Can you picture that? You move in for a kiss, catch wind of the vomit smell and end up throwing up on her. On the other hand, maybe she'll find it to be an emotionally bonding moment as you both puke together. All this talk of vomiting is making me sick to my stomach. I think I'm going to go puke.

Moral of the story: Live a healthy lifestyle for the right reasons. And make sure the "healthy" choices you are making are actually healthy.

CHAPTER 45

That's a Wrap

No matter how many people that I talk to, I'm still equally amazed every single day at the vibrant display of humiliating, embarrassing, ignorant fucks that make up the bottom-half of the gene pool. Until people begin to educate themselves, society will be creeping along the evolutionary ladder. We could be much farther technologically than we are, but there are so many ignorant and uneducated people out there, that it seems every time we take one step forward, we're forced to take two steps back.

It's not just the people out there that have no idea what religion they are, or why they chose to believe their religion. It's not just the wrongful indoctrination of society's bright future. It's not just racism and prejudice on every street of the world, or the hatred that stems from misunderstanding and a lack of tolerance among people. It's all of the above, and it's going to have to stop and some point.

I made my choice to make a change in the world when I decided to write this book. Please don't be one of the people that go on day after day blindly hating others. Stand up and make a change. If you want to trust in faith that God will send you a miracle, that's fine. Until that happens, do me a favor and be the miracle worker in His absence. Don't be afraid of what other people will say if you're different from them. I hope you've enjoyed this book, and I'm quite sure I will be receiving hate mail by the truckload when this is published.

I leave you all with one more thought. If I can get off of my fat ass and write a book in my leisure of time, while still going to school full-time, working nights full-time, and taking care of my two daughters, I know any one of you can do the same. You can probably even do it better. After all, I'm not even a writer, remember? I'm only one man. I only have one voice. But together, we can begin to spread the message that leads to a better tomorrow. We can build a society and a world where people can accept one another and work toward a common goal of a prosperous future. We owe it to ourselves. Don't do it for me. Do it for mankind. Do it for the future of our children.

Moral of the story: For God's sake, get off of the MOTHER-FUCKING COUCH PEOPLE!!!!!

FROM THE AUTHOR

Note To The World—If You Remember Nothing Else From This Book, Please Remember This:

> "I would rather be a pariah in a society of zombies, than be accepted for something that I'm not."

—Alex P. Hewing